WHO WILL SAVE ME FROM GRANDPA?

The Impact of 10 Years of Sexual Abuse at the Hands of My Grandfather and My Journey of Healing

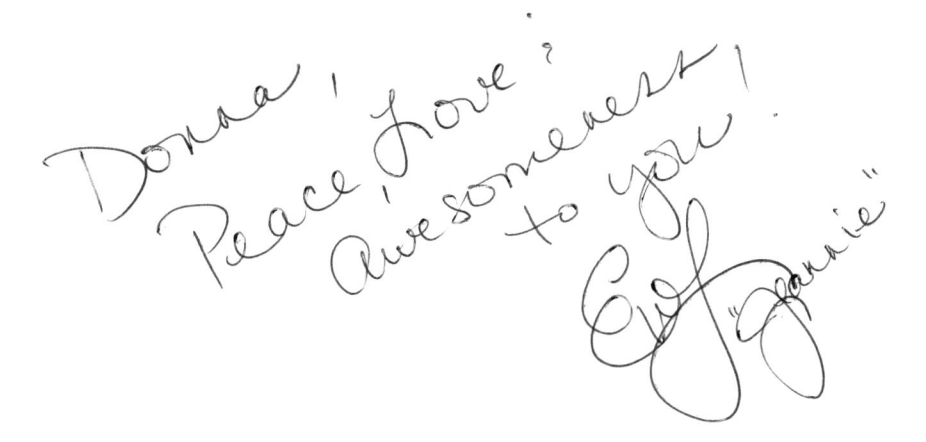

CARRIE WILLIAMS-LEE

authorHOUSE

AuthorHouse™
1663 Liberty Drive
Bloomington, IN 47403
www.authorhouse.com
Phone: 1 (800) 839-8640

© 2018 Carrie Williams-Lee. All rights reserved.

No part of this book may be reproduced, stored in a retrieval system, or transmitted by any means without the written permission of the author.

Published by AuthorHouse   06/20/2018

ISBN: 978-1-5462-4392-2 (sc)
ISBN: 978-1-5462-4390-8 (hc)
ISBN: 978-1-5462-4391-5 (e)

Library of Congress Control Number: 2018906335

Print information available on the last page.

Any people depicted in stock imagery provided by Getty Images are models, and such images are being used for illustrative purposes only.
Certain stock imagery © Getty Images.

This book is printed on acid-free paper.

Because of the dynamic nature of the Internet, any web addresses or links contained in this book may have changed since publication and may no longer be valid. The views expressed in this work are solely those of the author and do not necessarily reflect the views of the publisher, and the publisher hereby disclaims any responsibility for them.

Acknowledgments

Curtis, I give you my wholehearted gratitude for your love, support and understanding when I couldn't love, support or understand myself.

To Cordell, Dr. Brook, Nicole and Natalie: I am indebted to you for your genius, honesty, and assistance in editing my work. I hope I have blessed your life as much as you have mine through this process!

And, to all who loved me completely before I learned to love myself, I am eternally thankful for each one of you!

Carrie Williams-Lee

"I expect to pass through this world but once. Any good thing, therefore, that I can do or any kindness I can show to any creature, let me do it now. Let me not defer or neglect it, for I shall not pass this way again."

— Stephen Grellet

Contents

Chapter One
    Something a Child Should Never Have to Do
Chapter Two
    A Sheltered Childhood?
Chapter Three
    Ignorance is NOT Bliss
Chapter Four
    Stolen Firsts
Chapter Five
    Seeing Red
Chapter Six
    Our Little Secret
Chapter Seven
    Faith
Chapter Eight
    The Ugly Duckling and the Black Sheep
Chapter Nine
    Standing in Shadows
Chapter Ten
    The Promise
Chapter Eleven
    A Dark New Day
Chapter Twelve
    Rest in Pieces
Chapter Thirteen
    Into the Pit
Chapter Fourteen
    Easy Prey
Chapter Fifteen
    Positively Negative
Chapter Sixteen
    Help or Hindrance?
Chapter Seventeen
    The Broken Glass Is Half Full
Chapter Eighteen
    Learning to Be Worthy
Chapter Nineteen
    Gifts
Chapter Twenty
    Shades of Darkness
Chapter Twenty-One
    Darkness…
Chapter Twenty-Two
    …Into Light
Chapter Twenty-Three
    Negativity Breeds Negativity
Chapter Twenty-Four
    Revelations
Chapter Twenty-Five
    Exposure
Chapter Twenty-Six
    Peace, Love and Awesomeness

A Word from the Author

I hadn't put much thought into writing a book about my experiences regarding this subject matter until I received a phone call from a girlfriend of mine. She knew of the sexual abuse that I had suffered as a child and called me for advice. Her adult daughter had recently approached her and revealed to her that a family member had sexually abused her when she was a child. My friend was extremely distraught about this news and needed to seek some solace and direction, and she pleaded with me to help her make her next move. My words to her were simply *VALIDATE YOUR DAUGHTER*. I explained to her how important it is to take the information that her daughter provided her with and do whatever it took to show her daughter that her life is valuable and that she is worthy…that she *matters*.

My friend's daughter explained why she finally revealed the information after all of the years that she held it in for so long. She stated that she was exhausted by trying to conceal the abuse and was weary of being at family gatherings where she continued to be forced to face her abuser. Hearing this, I was aware that her daughter's abuser was still alive so I told her that the most important thing she could do is press charges against this man. Not only would this action help validate her daughter's worth but there is a good possibility that he has or is still victimizing others. Her answer absolutely appalled me…she could not press charges. She could not even approach her daughter's abuser because her husband, who is the brother of the abuser, made the dreadfully biased excuse, "We can't say or do anything about it because it will just destroy the family." In that moment I realized that my friend's daughter was not going to receive the justice she deserves. My friend and her husband did not consider the damage that had been done to their daughter's mind, body and soul from this agonizing secret she finally had found the immeasurable strength to reveal.

I informed my friend of treatment options that had helped me, giving her the names and phone numbers of facilities that I had utilized that had impacted my life positively. I filled my friend with as much first-hand information that I could in the hopes that it would help her daughter find some healing and peace.

I spoke to my friend several times regarding her daughter and we discussed the very dark places that her daughter had existed in for so many years. I attempted to be a resource and a co-healer who could possibly help lessen her daughter's suffering, but my actions to assist were not met with the fervor that I expected. Her daughter was left in a continuous state of torment and a life in a prison that I know too well.

I chose to write this book due to the fact that so many victims and families of victims are unaware of the vicious tolls sexual abuse takes on a victim's life, relationships and their mental and physical health. Sexual abuse is not a matter that one can just sweep under a rug and ignore in the hopes that it disappears. It compounds, it consumes and swallows the victim whole only to imprison them. It can lead to self-deprecating actions and lifestyles and can result in death.

My penning of this book was one designed to show how sexual abuse appeared in my life, how it has affected my mind and body and the journey I took to find healing.

By revealing personal, intimate and sometimes graphic information and experiences about myself, my desire is to help others out of the abyss created by this perversion. I hope to also introduce some understanding for those who have a loved one who has been a victim of sexual abuse.

I begin Chapters Three through Eleven with a vignette. These events are flashbacks of the actual sexual abuse that I suffered and have played in my head for decades, changing my views about the world around me from a very young age. Unknowingly, my mind placed all of these horrible things into the realm of "normal", and it was most definitely not. When this happens, a life is changed negatively and forever. These vignettes are void of the graphic details that I was required to write for exposure therapy. My hope is to show how ugly sexual abuse is. **It is NOT sex.** Imagine writing and reading these vignettes repetitively as exposure therapy as an adult and one can see how taxing and difficult exposure therapy can be. But it works. I am proof.

My journey of writing this book has been a very beneficial one. I have discovered that the combination of writing and the continuation of therapy during the process have been exceptionally revealing and healing for me. I truly believe it is the process that I was destined to experience in order to fulfill my ultimate purpose and help others find healing, whether the reader is a victim of sexual abuse, loved one of a victim or those who seek knowledge about how the atrocities of sexual abuse can play out in one's life.

I wish you healing, love and peace.

Chapter One

Something a Child Should Never Have to Do

"Come over here for a minute."

I heard this request many times before, but this time it was different.

Interrupted from my casual walk through the living room, I glance into the kitchen from where the request was made. On the other side of the aluminum-edged, yellow Formica peninsula that separates the dated kitchen from the living room, sits my grandfather.

He is a well groomed man with a full head of dark hair which he keeps neatly combed back and he always smells of Zest soap and aftershave. His gently lined face is rounded, but with a defined jaw line and chin.

Before I take a step towards him to honor his request, I pause and think to myself in my thirteen year old mind, *He has had a couple of strokes recently…and he has seemed to have forgotten a lot of things. Maybe he has forgotten about this, too.*

Hesitantly, I walk over to the man sitting on the perch from where he has beckoned for me many times before.

As I stand awkwardly in front of him, not knowing what to expect, he begins to touch be inappropriately.

He has NOT forgotten.

Suddenly, a powerful jolt of consciousness screams through my body as I grab his age spotted hand and forcefully pull it away from me. The unrestrained words explode from my mouth, "YOU CAN'T DO THIS TO ME ANYMORE!"

Frozen with shock from the powerful words that just exited my broken soul, I stand terrified of the repercussions of my perceived disrespect towards my grandfather.

"*You* know, *you* could have stopped it any time you wanted to," he replies.

Confusion courses through me. Time seems to stop as waves of intense emotion crash into me. I attempt to process what has just occurred. I struggle to take my next breath, silently maintain my newly acquired courage, and walk away from the kitchen chair where my grandfather is sitting. Ironically, this notorious chair is one of the frequent places from which he repetitively thieved my innocence over the past ten years.

This moment of immense life change passes, the clock restarts again, and we both move forward with our days, acting as if nothing extraordinary has just happened.

It was over.

Chapter Two

A Sheltered Childhood?

I was born on a warm spring day in late April in 1966, as the third child of a young couple in the Midwest. I was a welcome addition to my two older brothers; three year old Calvin and one and a half year old Craig. I was an adorable little blonde-haired, curly-headed little girl with great big blue eyes.

***

Cathy is my mom. She is a tall woman with a beautifully sculpted face, kind blue eyes and a genuine and beautiful smile. She has worn her light brown hair in short styles for as long as I can remember. I used to like watching her use the old-fashioned "rollers" to set her hair after she would wash it. She would use a rat tail comb, part each section, put the curler in and use a plastic pin to keep the curler in place. Magically, in the morning, she removed the brush-like curlers and her hair was curled! She wasn't blessed with the head full of ringlets that I have always had. Mom always told me those I got from my Dad, since he has some waviness to his hair.

Mom is the elder sister to two younger brothers produced within the marriage of my grandfather and my grandmother. She also has a half-brother from my grandmother's first marriage. I never knew him because he suddenly passed away when he was seventeen years old.

She was raised in a very devout Catholic family and attended parochial school. She was reared with typical "1950s" idealism; a woman is to marry, bear children, raise said children, and be an efficient homemaker, loving wife, and caring mother.

Ken is my dad. He is a handsome man with rounded facial features and a prematurely gray, receding hairline. My childhood memories of my remarkably brilliant dad are of him as the provider of food and home who went to work each day to take care of his kids and his wife.

Who Will Save Me from Grandpa?

Much like the "Ward Cleaver" type of father, he was always quick with a word of advice and with discipline when needed.

Mom was never opposed to doling out punishment but I would tremble when she used the phrase, "YOU JUST WAIT 'TIL YOUR FATHER GETS HOME!" I would sit in my bedroom, where I had been sequestered for whatever dirty deed I had just committed, waiting...and waiting. When I would hear the front door open at exactly 5:30 pm, my ever-increasing anxiety would overwhelm me. While I nervously strained to hear my Mom inform him of my crime, he would sternly walk into my room, take his belt off and ready it for delivering my sentence. He had a way of looping his belt and pulling on it with both hands to make a loud "slap" before using it for swatting my behind. That would scare the crap out of me and I think it made the spanking hurt worse than it really did. Like I was always forewarned, I really do think it hurt Dad more than it hurt me.

I mentioned that my dad is brilliant, but he's also very skilled at many trades. He was forever building elaborate gadgets, fixing whatever might be broken, and volunteering his limitless skills to help other people. Many times he would arm himself with a soldering iron and a collection of tiny circuitry parts and settle down at the kitchen table to construct circuit boards for who-knows-what. I enjoyed watching the distinctively scented solder smoke rise from his solder gun and watch all of those little parts become something, even though I had no clue what it was.

Dad is the eldest of two boys and was raised in a single parent household. His dad had left his mom for another woman and played no part in either boy's upbringing. Dad never really spoke of his childhood, which made him somewhat mysterious to me. From the few stories I have heard about his childhood, I don't think it was a happy one.

Being a cute little girl and the youngest of three children had its benefits; I wasn't just the center of attention at times, but also the center of big messes. I am told that Cal and Craig adored me and would cover me with kisses. They also managed to cover me, themselves and the bedroom where I was napping with baby powder while innocently "taking care of" their baby sister. I am sure that their little white,

Chapter 2 ~ A Sheltered Childhood?

powdery faces staring at my mom upon her discovery made it difficult for her to scold them.

Once I was somewhat older, I would join in with my brothers to make messes, like peeling all of the labels off of the cans of food in the cupboard. Mom would have to open "mystery cans" and hope that inside was something that would go with the meal she prepared.

For the first two years of my life, our young family lived in a small brick bungalow just south of the city. It was a suburb where my mother spent her childhood. Although I was very young, I still have flashes of memories of my mother packing to move to a new house. Even at the age of two, I can remember her throwing away a stuffed skunk toy that someone had given her as a gift for me before I was even born. Jokingly, I have given her trouble about pitching that skunk. She swears the thing was falling apart but I still act like I miss it.

In 1968, we moved to a town that was still landscaped with cornfields, but urban sprawl had started to make its mark with shiny new subdivisions and spacious homes being built at a rapid pace. Twenty miles or more south of the city seemed to be a desirable distance away from industrialization and close enough to "country" to achieve the American Dream and raise a proper family.

Mom valued being a wife and a mother and her ultimate goal was to raise her kids with the proper standards and values that she was taught. In order to do this, she chose to be a stay-at-home mom during a time when it seemed many other moms went to work each day.

Mom stretched pennies instead of dollars. There were no frills to be had, just necessities. Due to Mom's savvy for saving money, our family was perceived by others as being affluent. As a kid, I didn't know differently. Hand-me-downs, garage sales, couponing and being strict about saying "NO" to all of the incessant cries of "I want…" from us kids kept our family in a nice, comfortable home.

As I saw it, we seemed to be the picture perfect American family: a "stay at home" mom and a dad who worked a 9 to 5 job. Dad would arrive after work to an immaculate house with a kiss for his bride and then sit down to a tasty home-cooked meal on the table where every evening we ate dinner as a family.

Who Will Save Me from Grandpa?

My parents were exceptionally protective regarding my brothers and me. They were very strict about what they exposed us to as kids, making sure we only viewed "G" rated movies and even limited the cartoons that we watched on Saturday mornings. I still tease them about not allowing us kids to watch *Scooby Doo* cartoons because they thought they were "bad". We never spent a whole lot of time in front of the television but when we did, it was something wholesome, such as *The Wonderful World of Disney* or *The Brady Bunch*.

My parents were determined to keep their kids from any kind of malevolence. They sheltered us from profanity, events or conversations that might strip our innocence from us. They kept any bickering or fighting between the two of them private.

My vocabulary was limited only to what I heard and was taught at school. I was encouraged to avoid making friends with "questionable" children, usually pointed out to me by Mom. I thought she had some kind of super power when it came to knowing which kids were good and which ones were bad so I heeded her warnings.

In spite of the sheltered world my parents lovingly created for me, evil had a slick way of entering in…through the family; disguised as a grandpa.

I was only taught to "beware of strangers". I was never taught to beware of people who are supposed to love me and protect me.

While in the care of my grandparents, my grandfather began sexually abusing me when I was three years old. My earliest recollection of the abuse is receiving a gift that my grandparents had recently brought back from a vacation in Florida. I was handed a small sack of bright orange gum balls that resembled a bag of oranges and I was thrilled to be given a treat.

Then, I just know "something" happened.

Through ages four and five, the abuse continued and signs of the abuse began surfacing. Severe kidney infections that made me extremely ill, painful bladder infections, limited bladder control, bedwetting, and crying from the intense burning I felt when I would urinate, were all clues of the physical damage that was being done to my small body.

Chapter 2 ~ A Sheltered Childhood?

Once my parents sought treatment for these chronic issues I was having, my doctor informed my parents I would be required to spend a few days in a hospital for some tests and for a procedure that possibly needed to be done.

I was placed in a room that already had someone in another bed. She introduced herself as Carrie Nichols. I thought she was cool because I had never met anyone with my first name before! Plus, her last name was Nichols…just like the coin that I learned was worth five cents!

I was given a short hospital gown adorned with little yellow ducklings to wear on my five-year-old frame. The gown customarily tied in back and left my backside uncovered.

The nurses, who were Catholic nuns, kept me busy coloring and playing "nurse" with them when my parents weren't there with me. I waddled around in my duckie–covered gown through the hospital helping them deliver foam pitchers of water to their other patients. Not being aware of modesty at that age, I gave little thought to my little rear end peeking through the back of my gown for all to see.

My parents would come to visit, but my brothers were forbidden to go further into the hospital than the front lobby due to their young ages, so they would bring my Grandma Williams along to watch the boys. Dad would later go down to the lobby to relieve Grandma so she could come to my room and visit.

I did not know that going to the hospital would be so fun and that I would get presents! My grandma brought Sunshine Fun Family dolls, which were all the rage in the early 1970s, along with some other gifts to keep me occupied while I was there.

The nun-nurses would routinely come to my room, make me drink some vile liquid, position me atop a cold, metal bed pan and then hand me bubble wrap to pop while we waited for me to urinate. In retrospect, I am sure it wasn't very pleasant for my adult roommate to listen to the POP! POP! POP! of a five-year-old enjoying her first experience with bubble wrap.

The test results were inconclusive regarding the cause of my symptoms, and the treatment that was deemed necessary was to have my urethra "stretched", as Mom tells me. This was to be done while I was under general anesthesia so I was not allowed to eat or drink anything prior to the procedure, which seemed like forever as a five-year-old.

My nice roommate had brought me back a small package of red licorice from the vending machine. (In my five-year-old mind, I imagined she paid for with nickels because of her last name.) I never really liked that particular candy, and I had only eaten a very small bite of it when I mentioned to my mom over the phone that I had done so. She promptly reminded me that I wasn't to be eating anything, so I abided and stuck nothing more in my mouth.

I was taken to a room where the procedure was to be done and the nurse assisted me from my comfy hospital bed to a cold, stainless steel table. Once on top of the table, I was asked to scoot down to help reposition me for the procedure and when I did, my bare butt made a funny squeaking noise that made me and the doctors giggle.

Once the procedure was finished and I awoke from the anesthesia, I suffered from severe nausea and vomiting as a side effect. Suddenly, hospitals were no longer fun.

Although I exhibited the proper signs that pointed towards the strong possibility I was being sexually abused, the subject of sexual abuse or incest was taboo. At the time, even the hospital staff did not consider sexual abuse as a causative factor for the conditions that afflicted me, despite the evidence.

Chapter Three

Ignorance is NOT Bliss

"Fish Stories"

It is a stormy summer day, and a greenish-grey sky threatens more thunderstorms. With weather like this, it is not a good day to use the lake or play outside, so my grandfather and I settle in for a day under cover, away from the rain.

Directly underneath the noisy window air conditioning unit, my grandfather sits at a square, gray card table in the screened-in porch. He is sorting through his tackle box, readying some fishing lures, rods and reels for his next trip to catch "the big one".

I am sitting cross-legged on the floor in front of him as he tells me stories. As I listen intently to him, he explains to me the finer points of a particular extra-marital affair he has had with a nurse. Somehow, it did not seem strange to me that my grandfather was telling me that he had been spending time with another woman.

He explains to me how he uses "rubbers" when he has sexual relations with this woman so he does not contract a disease. In my immature mind, I picture a black rubber hose, like the ones I have seen my dad install near the engines of cars.

I try to imagine a black rubber hose covering his private part and wonder how that would prevent him from getting a disease. Nonetheless, I continue to listen attentively.

He finishes his story-telling and he calls me to him. I stand up and walk a few feet to him.

Yep. It is happening again and I just let him. I stand there confused as always as I distance my mind from the current events. What he is doing to me makes me feel weird and dirty, I know it will eventually be over, so I focus on that.

My anxiety is heightened and I worry that we will be seen as he exploits me on the porch where anyone who might stop by could see us. Added to the overwhelming anxiety is the dread that my grandmother will discover us, since she is just inside the house.

Who Will Save Me from Grandpa?

He completes his method of tutoring me by pulling his handkerchief out of his pocket, soiling it as he finishes.

We then casually go about our day.

My mother's parents lived about sixty miles south of the city in a lake community. They had purchased their retirement home there in the late 1960's and moved after living the first part of their married life in the city. It was a small, two bedroom house with a large screened-in patio that sat on a hill overlooking the lake. It seemed to be the perfect place to take the grandkids to spend time fishing, swimming, and visiting.

For as long as I had known my grandmother, she was afflicted with several health conditions, and she relied on a wheelchair for mobility. She had severely arthritic knees that made walking extremely painful and difficult. Her day usually consisted of sitting in her recliner and watching television. Sometimes she would nap while in her chair or go into her bedroom to watch TV and sleep. She loved watching soap operas (she referred to them as "her stories"), and we knew to be quiet when they were on. My grandfather, on the other hand, was mobile and was able to take care of my grandma. When he wasn't taking care of her, he kept himself busy by fishing and hunting. There was always fresh fish, rabbit and squirrel meat to fill our bellies with when we visited.

Each summer, Mom saw it fit to send me to my grandparents' house for weeks at a time to "help" around their house, which usually meant there was some kind of cleaning job that needed to be done. I suppose my mom also thought of it as sort of a vacation for me because I could go swimming and fishing in the lake. Most of the time, I would stay at their house by myself. Occasionally, my cousin or my brothers would visit at the same time I was staying.

Most weekends, Mom felt it was her duty to travel to their house and take care of her folks. This was family time for us; a time to visit, a time for us kids to wander around the lake, a time to spend the day fishing or hiking into the woods or going to the "dump" and sifting through others' garbage that community members brought there to be eventually burned in rusty, charred barrels. I recall the lingering

Chapter 3 ~ Ignorance is NOT Bliss

smell of burnt trash on some of the items that my brothers and I would proudly cart back to my grandparents house, only to have Mom or Dad make us dispose of the "junk" that we had found. What we thought was a prize as kids was evidently worthless rubbish to the adults.

I would spend many hours on the large, screened-in patio that overlooked the lake. I used to like watching thunderstorms roll in while we sat on the white painted metal patio furniture that sported bright green, yellow and orange flowered cushions. With lightening cracking and thunder rumbling, rain would pour all around and I could feel the change in the atmosphere while I stayed dry while under the shelter of the patio. It was a very popular place for the whole family. Kids and adults alike would have their tackle boxes open with hooks and lures spilling out of them. The patio gave us ample room to play, prepare for a day of fishing, and visit with each other.

Aluminum screened doors served as three different entry and exit points for the screened in patio, one on each green screened wall. The poured concrete floor was covered with a very short pile, dark green indoor/outdoor carpet where I gained several good rug burns from horsing around with my brothers. From the patio, the wooden entry door into the house had a diamond-shaped glass window at an adult's eye level for peering out. Before the entrance to the house, there was a small, closet-like room that functioned as a storage room and a laundry room. This room was very dimly lit and had a distinctive odor of laundry detergent and of the old cardboard boxes that were stacked on the shelves above the washer and dryer.

My grandfather had an affinity for luxury cars and there was always one parked under the adjacent carport. A shiny, black Cadillac made way for a brand new, big, brown Buick Electra. As kids, we were fascinated by the power windows in this fancy car. We would roll the windows up and down repetitively until we were scolded to stop.

Other amenities that the car boasted were ashtrays with flip-up lids. Once the ashtray lid was flipped up, there was a cigarette lighter that we liked to press down to activate. Once it "popped" back up, we would pull it out and be amazed at the hot, glowing coils, always with a warning to not burn ourselves. (Of course we burned ourselves, but

Who Will Save Me from Grandpa?

we wouldn't dare say a word!) There was a flip-down armrest in the center of the rear seat that we kids would fight over because it made us taller in the seat.

Holidays were times that my grandparents' whole house would be packed with family. My mom's brothers would join us with their families to share a good meal and a lot of laughs. My uncles were very humorous and would keep us all in stitches.

We always looked forward to spending Easter at their house. At the community park within the lake development, an Easter egg hunt would be held every year. My brothers and my younger cousin, Deanna, would race to see who could find the most eggs and win the most prizes. Once the festivities at the park were over, we would then go back to my grandparents' house for the traditional Easter ham and brag about our winnings.

Deanna was a cute, blonde haired, green-eyed little girl; fun-loving, quick witted like her father, and always a people pleaser. She was an only child to my aunt and uncle for ten years until her sister was born. I was glad when Deanna would be at our grandparents' house at when I was. She was as close to a sister that I had and we enjoyed each other as playmates.

Mom's youngest brother had three daughters. Due to our age difference, I spent more time babysitting them when I was a teenager than I spent childhood play time with them. They were my "little" cousins and I did not build relationships with them until adulthood.

Deanna's parents would send her down to our grandparents' house during the summers, as well. It was nice when we could be there at the same time. Although we were always given chores to do, they were less tedious doing them together.

I suppose my parents saw sending me down to their house as a vacation for me, kind of like summer camp. I have always loved to swim, and I liked to fish, so I spent a lot of time at the lake. It was a place where I could explore and create my own adventures by myself and sometimes with Deanna or my brothers. My parents' desire for me to spend quality time with my grandparents and starting me on the path to being a "caretaker", much like my mother, seemed innocent enough.

Chapter 3 ~ Ignorance is NOT Bliss

I was expected to complete chores using my childish hands and immature mind, usually with my grandma barking, "Use more elbow grease!" Polishing the chrome dining chair legs until they gleamed, cleaning the fronts of the kitchen cabinets and then conditioning them by applying Liquid Gold ever-so-carefully, cleaning out mothball scented closets with families of silverfish squirming around in them, helping my grandma take a bath, and painting metal patio furniture are just a small list of the tasks I was given to complete.

I guess helping my grandparents was designed to have some redeeming virtue. I did these things because that is what was expected of me. I loved my parents and my grandparents, and in my world, these things were what good granddaughters did. Nonetheless, what I gained from these "lessons in life" was much more than instilling work ethics or learning how to be charitable. While I was fulfilling my parents wishes, and in their minds, getting to know my grandparents and being nurtured and protected while in their custody, my life was being permanently and negatively changed.

My grandfather would lure me away from the family by asking me to go for a seemingly innocent car ride, maybe a trip to the store or just a short fishing trip to the lake. My parents always gave me permission to accompany him, believing I would be protected by my grandfather while I was out of their sight. I felt special because he chose *me* over the other kids to be by his side.

As I got a little older, I began having certain feelings about what he was doing to me. The things he was doing to my body, what he was teaching me, and what I had to witness started to feel uncomfortable for me physically, mentally and spiritually.

Chapter Four
Stolen Firsts

"Having a Sleepover at Grandma's and Grandpa's House"

The sun has set, darkness has settled in and another summer day at my grandparents' house has come to an end. I slip my favorite "night gown" on, which is one of my dad's well-worn t-shirts, proper with tiny holes in it. I swim in the fabric as I am a young girl, but it is my daddy's shirt, which holds with it a comforting factor. I say good-night to my grandparents and head to the bedroom that I sleep in when I stay the night at their house.

Their house is a small, two bedroom home, which is plenty of room for the two of them. They share the master bedroom, each having their own twin sized bed on opposite sides of the room. The second bedroom is the perfect place for guests to sleep when they stay over. The room is furnished with two twin beds, separated by a nightstand with a lamp that sits on it. The aroma of moth balls seeps from under the closet doors, which lightly fragrances the bedroom with its unmistakable scent.

I prefer the bed that is closest to the door because it is underneath the big painting of a lake with a water-worn wooden boat and family of ducks floating on its misty water. I refuse to sleep in the other bed because I had once found a dead spider between the sheets and there is a window above it that might allow for more to creep in.

I snuggle into bed and close my eyes, dreaming of what fun and exciting things I might do the following day at the lake. I quickly fall into slumber.

My sleep is abruptly interrupted by my grandfather, who is wearing only his white briefs. He has waited for my grandmother to fall asleep so he can lurk around the house and prowl into the bedroom where I am sleeping, which is situated right next to their room.

In the dim light of the moon that leaches through the curtains, he instructs me to be silent and for me to remove my panties so he can do unspeakable things to me. I have no understanding of what he is telling me, especially since I was awakened from a deep sleep and I am groggy.

I lay there, frenzied with confusion. My young mind cannot comprehend why

Chapter 4 ~ Stolen Firsts

anyone would want to do these weird things to parts of my body. I stare bewildered at the shadowy ceiling as he continues to introduce me to another act in his repertoire, followed by the infamous handkerchief.

He finishes his nightmarish violation of me and exits the room. I slip my panties back on so I can curl up and go back to sleep.

Many of the normal rites of passage of a young girl were perversely stolen from me. Robbed from me was the innocence of many things. My right to remain a child and to not behold or experience the disgusting events in which I was forced to partake in was stripped away from me, forever leaving an indelible mark in my mind, severely damaging my thought process and how I viewed the world around me.

Having a conversation with girlfriends has always been difficult when the topic turned to "first kisses" and the like. Girls should have memories that conjure up only sweet, innocent feelings about their first kiss. In my distorted experience, the seemingly innocent topic was a traumatic event that I continue to relive over and over again through flashbacks. The smell of his aftershave and the horrid taste of his rancid denture breath is my memory of my corrupted first kiss.

One summer day, during one of my many visits to my grandparent's house, I glanced upward and across the green carpeted living room towards the second bedroom where I usually slept when I stayed. Much to my surprise, there stood my grandfather, who was completely nude! As I stared reluctantly at his hairy, potbellied, sixty-something body, he attempted to educate me: "This is what a grown man looks like!"

My grandmother was asleep in the very next room, just feet away from where he stood in his gratuitous nakedness. His brazen theft of another "first" from me has burned the image of his revolting, naked body into my mind and corrupted yet another experience for me.

Somewhere near the age of nine, my mother had "the talk" with me. She attempted to educate me about the "birds and the bees" when she noticed I had started developing breasts. Armed with a brochure that showed a graph of the stages of ovulation, she sat me on the living room couch and fingered awkwardly through the brochure. As she attempted to highlight the finer points of menstruation she affirmed,

~ 15 ~

"When a husband and wife love each other…", then in no specific terms I was told a baby is made. There was no mention of sexual intercourse, no mention of sperm fertilizing an ovum and no words referring to sexual organs or how they function. I was also told that eventually I would begin "bleeding".

Not too long after "the talk", my mother informed me and my brothers that she was pregnant.

I was down at my grandparents' house during the early part of summer before my brother, Corey, was born. One morning, I was sitting next to my grandfather at our all-too-familiar spot at the table. He questions me, "You know how your mom got pregnant, don't you?"

I sort of understood that people had to "do something" to make a baby. In my nine-year-old mind, whatever it is they had to do they only did once, creating a reserve of little "baby seeds" in the mother's body. Once God decided it was time for that couple to have another baby, the baby seeds would ripen, which is exactly what I innocently told him.

"NO! Your mom and dad had sex," and went on to tell me step by step what they had been doing.

I knew what his description of the acts he was describing all too well.

I was extremely sickened by this thought. As a child I never connected that repulsive act with reproduction. The matter-of-fact education I received that day from my grandfather replaced my sweet and innocent nine-year-old idea of how "babies are made" with perverse visuals and thoughts.

Chapter Five

Seeing Red

On a Sunday during the summer of 1975, much like most Sundays throughout the year, my family and I traveled down to my grandparents' house to spend the day swimming, fishing and visiting. This warm summer day, about a month before my tenth birthday, was perfect for the yellow polyester shorts that I paired with the handmade sleeveless blouse with multicolored miniature flower print and drawstring-gathered-neckline that tied in a bow. It was one of my favorite outfits.

At some point during our visit at my grandparents' house, my grandfather asked me to go fishing with him on his pontoon boat. My brothers were involved in another activity, so just I was going to accompany him. I asked my parents' permission, which of course, they gave.

We grabbed our fishing gear and headed to the dock where his pontoon boat was floating.

My grandfather then untied the boat and headed out to find the perfect place to cast some lines and fish. His boat was not fancy in any way. He had purchased it pre-owned and it basically just served the purpose of a fishing platform; kind of a mobile dock. It was not embellished with any kind of seating or canopies and in order to have a seat to fish we would have to sit on a folding chair.

As I stood on the pontoon boat holding the cork handle of my freshly cast fishing rod; the line's hook baited with an ill-fated worm, I fixed my stare towards the bobber to catch sight of any signs of a bite. My grandfather, who was seated on a folding chair on the other side of the boat, summoned me to his familiar side.

He had anchored the pontoon boat in a tree-shaded spot not too far from the edge of the lake and near some unoccupied docks. Undoubtedly, we were within eyesight from anyone that might be in their back yards or peering through the back windows of the row of homes that graced the shore of the lake. Taking no concern of this fact, my grandfather began doing to me what he usually did in private. I was embarrassed and fretted that people would see what we were doing. Once he was finished with his vile act, he continued fishing and then we returned to the house where my parents were, where we both acted as if nothing had happened.

That evening, once we were home, my brothers and I settled down on the floor in front of the television to watch *The Wonderful World of Disney*, as we did at 6:00 pm every Sunday. Facing the television, the three of us lied side by side on our bellies atop the large green sculpted rug that covered the living room floor, with our heads propped up on our hands above our bent elbows. Mom was sitting on the couch against the wall several feet behind us. She gathered my attention and directed me to follow her into the bathroom. We entered the bathroom and she sat down on the closed toilet seat as I stood before her. She then spun me around as if I was trying on a fancy new dress. Confused about what this was about, she then exclaimed, "Yep! That's what I thought!"

As I looked down to try to make sense out of what she was saying, I was stunned and horrified to see my yellow polyester shorts shrieking with bright red blood coming from my crotch area. I knew what my grandfather had done to me that day and I assumed he had caused this to happen. I burst out in tears and cried uncontrollably. My stomach sickened, the sharp pressure in my chest shot into my head while I internally screamed with pure fear. I was mortified that my mother would discover my secret and I would be severely punished for taking part in such sordid behavior.

My mother then explained to me that I had started my period, referring to "the talk" we had had not too long before then.

My mother then gently helped clean me up as I continued to sob. She then presented me with a huge, "old-fashioned" sanitary pad to secure onto my underwear with safety pins. I felt like I had an enormous diaper stuffed precariously between my legs.

Ashamed and apprehensive, I walked back into the living room where my brothers were still positioned in the same place that I left them; propped up in front of the television. I prayed that neither one of

Chapter 5 ~ Seeing Red

them had seen the blood and could not detect this giant wad of cotton-like material attached to my underwear.

Since we visited my grandparents frequently, I soon faced my grandfather. He managed to get me alone again and mentioned to me that my mom had informed him that I had "become a woman" and started my period. In a congratulatory manner he told me that my vagina "felt wider open" that day to him.

This marked change in my life was still very raw and I was distressed about the situation. It was disconcerting to discuss this topic with anyone, particularly my grandfather. Hearing his comments only exacerbated my anguish.

I now had something new to cause me added distress and anxiety; the possibility of getting pregnant at nine years old by my grandfather.

Chapter Six

Our Little Secret

"Just Hanging Out and Reading Magazines"

Like most summers, I am visiting my grandparents' to spend time with them and help them out where I can with chores around their house, or at least what I can do at the age of nine.

On this particular day, my grandfather asks me to get into his car, which is parked under a metal roofed concrete pad that cantilevers off the side of the screened in patio. The bright summer sun casts a sharply defined shadow under the carport, making it a comfortably cool spot on this warm day. I assume we are going somewhere, so I open the driver's side door and slide onto the smooth, bench-style brown leather seat and scoot towards the passenger side and my grandfather seats himself on the driver's seat.

He asks me to move closer to him. I feel confused when he does not put his keys into the ignition and instead, opens up a magazine, flips through a few pages, finds the page he wants me to look at and hands it to me.

I feel the slick pages and the weight of the magazine in my childish hands as I hold it. The pictures in the magazine illustrate twin girls who are completely nude, except for their different colored 1970s style striped tube socks that are only worn so these twins can be distinguished from one another. The pictures glare back at me as these blonde twins are demonstrating things that I have never seen two girls do to each other.

My innocent eyes are peering upon something that is clearly wrong and it makes me feel "icky"; flushed and awkward, the heightened fight or flight reaction added to the intensifying anxiety of getting caught.

As I hold the magazine, my grandfather then begins his routine of molesting my small body.

Meanwhile, my nine year old mind is trying to process why my grandfather is sitting there next to me doing these things, knowing my grandmother is just inside

Chapter 6 ~ Our Little Secret

the house. I worry about her opening the side door of the house to look out and see what we are doing. Or does she already know?

Finally, the handkerchief comes out.

Symbolically, my grandfather pulling his handkerchief out of his pocket means that this is almost over; his release equals my relief.

He stuffs his repetitively soiled handkerchief back in his pocket, where he always keeps it. I close the magazine and hand it back to him. We exit the car and walk back into the screened in porch, where he enters the laundry room and places the magazine back into a cardboard box on the top shelf.

We go about the rest of our day as normal, behaving as if nothing out of the ordinary for any grandfather and granddaughter has occurred.

While other little girls were establishing sweet, unadulterated memories of spending time with their grandparents, and cherishing the special, loving relationship that is customary between a grandparent and a grandchild, I was attempting to decipher the special kind of "love" that I received from my grandfather.

During the years the sexual abuse occurred, my thoughts about what my grandfather was doing to me transitioned from normalcy to awareness that something about it wasn't quite right. Increasing feelings of shame, fear, and confusion engulfed me while the acts were occurring. I had an unspoken subservience to him. He told me it was "our secret" and I was not to tell anyone about what he was doing to me. Never once did he threaten me or tell me that something bad would happen if I revealed the secret. My lack of self-confidence and fear of punishment for not being obedient certainly influenced my silence.

For years after the abuse ended, I was plagued by countless flashbacks of the events. These flashbacks consumed my mind and controlled me well into my forties, until I finally found effective therapy that helped fade them.

The recurring flashbacks were commonplace in my daily life, like a non-stop reel of sickening movies that I was forced to star in.

The sexual abuse, coupled with the fear of being caught and the punishment I would endure if our deeds were found out, caused me ever-increasing anxiety. I had a healthy respect for punishment and did my best to stay out of trouble. This apprehension consumed my mind every day of my childhood life, not just when the molestation was occurring.

It seems my grandfather was aroused by the risky theatres in which he chose to abuse me. As blatant as he was at carrying out his crimes, many times with my own family just in the next room, I was never safe anywhere that he was. He was even brazen enough to approach me at my own home.

I find it questionable that these attacks at my grandfather's hand were unseen by all, considering there were at least two child victims; my cousin Deanna and I. Considering many of these offenses occurred in the confinements of their home with my grandmother in the adjacent room, it is curious that she was not aware of these events. Due to her health and disabilities, she was completely reliant on my grandfather, and should she admit to the crimes he was committing, she would have ended up alone.

Chapter Seven

Faith

"Summer Sports"

It is another warm summer day at my grandparents' house on the lake. Like most summer days I spend there, my plan for the day is to go swimming in the lake. Summer is my absolute favorite time of the year because I love swimming. I inform my grandfather of my hopes to spend time splashing around in the lake and he obliges.

Normally, my grandfather would drive me down to the swimming area and sit on a bench that was centered on the beach and supervise my play in the water, but today was different. He informs me that he is going to go swimming with me.

With swimming suits on and towels in hand, we climb into my grandfather's car and drive across the spillway, over the dam and arrive at the large swimming area at the lake.

It is a warm, somewhat overcast day. The swimming area is full of kids and adults, enjoying the cool water, building sand castles or jumping off of the diving board that is affixed to a concrete dock in the deep end.

My grandfather and I set our belongings down on the beach. We make our way down the sand and into the water. We head towards the right side of the swimming area, which is demarcated by staggered rusty metal barrels floating between lengths of rope. He stands for a time in the water as I swim around him, splashing and playing like any little kid.

I swim towards my grandfather, who is standing up to his neck in the cool lake water. He is a man about 6 feet tall, so the water being to his neck meant that I could not stand in this depth of water. He grabs me and has me wrap my arms around his neck as he proceeds to sexually abuse me under the water while I am clinging to his neck. People are swimming all around us. I fret that they will see what he is doing to me. I am wondering why no one even notices there is a man molesting his granddaughter right in front of them. I am looking around with apprehension, my heart pounding inside my chest wall, consumed with extremely heightened anxiety, hoping no one notices or I will have to explain all of this and I do not understand it myself.

~ 23 ~

Who Will Save Me from Grandpa?

Most of all, I fear being punished for allowing him do these atrocities to me, but I also fear retribution from him for not obeying.

Just like all of the other times, I know that this will be over once he "finishes". He doesn't' rely on the handkerchief this time since he is neck deep in the lake water.

I am sickened but I am glad it is over...so I can swim.

He exits the lake and perches himself on the bench he usually supervises my swimming from. I continue to swim and play in the water while he watches from the beach as he dries himself off with his towel.

I was raised in the Catholic faith until I was ten years old, attending Sunday school and church regularly, taking part in Holy Communion and Confession and the other rites of passage. Soon after I turned ten, my parents chose to leave the Catholic religion. They had heard the Word of Salvation and chose to find a church that preached more accordingly as Born Again Christians. Dad never seemed content in his search for a home church after that and we went from church to church and religion to religion. I chose not to get involved in activities or people at the churches because I figured we wouldn't be there very long.

Regardless of Dad's persistent hunt for the perfect church, faith in God the Father and Jesus as Our Savior was exemplified by my parents. Prayer, reading Scripture, and encouraging our faith surrounded all that our family did from saying Grace before dinner or the laying on of hands with prayer for healing.

My families' faith was the center of our lives regardless of a religious affiliation.

I suppose my parents' faith is one reason it was so easy to overlook the possibility of one of their children being sexually abused. They prayed for their children's safety and walked in faith that God would protect them. They certainly would never expect a family member to harm one of their children in any way, especially since they were people of faith, too.

Why look for signs of child sexual abuse when their unwavering faith was supposed to be protecting me from the wickedness of the world?

Chapter Eight

The Ugly Duckling and the Black Sheep

"Going to the Store with Grandpa"

I see that my grandfather has a shopping list and he asks me to go to the store with him. I get in my grandfather's car, and we head off to the store with hopes that I might get to shop for a new box of breakfast cereal or some kind of tasty treat.

As we ride down the road together, I stare out the passenger window with my only focus on the possibility of scoring a sweet candy bar or a box of sugary cereal.

My dream of indulgence is interrupted by the request to scoot across the long, bench style car seat nearer to my grandfather. I comply, as my obedient nature always does. He begins his immoral attack while haphazardly driving.

Panic consumes my mind as cars and trucks pass by us on the highway. I agonize over the chance that someone will see what we are doing. The overwhelming concern that we will be discovered displaces the realization of much of what he is doing to me in the car. This is the standard for many of our trips to the store, with an occasional added stop at a roadside park so my grandfather would not have to be bothered with driving while he defiles my immature body.

The anxiety eases as he removes the emblematic white handkerchief out of his pocket. My goal of getting that treat that I am hoping for at the store is now right around the corner.

When I look back on my childhood, I see it in sort of a bittersweet and confusing way, as if I lived a double life. I created many good memories with my family and a handful of childhood friends, but my recollection of these "enjoyable" times are cloaked in the depression, self-loathing and desire to die that I suffered as a child, which has made these memories seem as though I was only half-present in them. Because of these feelings, I never felt I fit in…anywhere.

My brother Craig was an attractive, extremely witty, kind hearted, and an exceptionally artistically talented child. He exemplifies these traits as an adult, carrying these qualities into his marriage and fatherhood. He has always been the comic relief in the family. No matter what kind of trouble he would get himself into, Dad would always have a hard time following through with his punishment because Craig would have him laughing so hard.

Since Craig and I are closer in age, we spent more time together playing as young kids than Cal and I did. We would set up my Barbie camper and his Big Jim camper, and we would send our dolls on an exciting excursion. After pushing our respective campers around the house, a campsite would be settled upon and then set up. Barbie would sit around the molded plastic campfire in her white go-go boots and groovy bell-bottomed jumpsuit, while Big Jim would crawl into his yellow vinyl sleeping bag and sleep under the imaginary stars.

My brother, Cal, was the logical and intellectual one. He was the epitome of the "first-born child"; always an over-achiever, striving for perfection in all facets of life. As he entered his teen years, I became his pesky little sister, and he did not seem to have a lot of time or patience for me. Because of the way I felt about myself, I believed that he hated me. There were three critical years between us and it was just enough for him to be in a different life stage that I didn't really fit into. As the years went by, Cal and I grew closer. When he began driving he would ask me to accompany him to go clothes shopping because he wanted a girl's opinion of what he was buying. During one trip to the mall, I persuaded Cal into signing for me to have my ear lobes double-pierced since he was eighteen. (Isn't that what big brothers are for?) When we returned home and our folks saw my new piercings, they were less than pleased with us.

Cal allowed me to wear his white nylon baseball jacket from high school that sported a big red number fifteen and the name "Williams" sewn onto the back. He was in college by then and wasn't wearing it anyway. I was so proud to wear this jacket of my brother's! I wore it constantly because it felt like a big hug from my brother, and of course I thought it made me cool, or at least I hoped it did.

I realized that once Cal and I finally became "buddies" and our

Chapter 8 ~ The Ugly Duckling and the Black Sheep

relationship changed, he had always loved his little sister; he just had a different way of showing it when we were kids.

Although Cal married and moved to another state, the few times a year I do get to see him, I still gaze upon him with admiration, and I treasure the transformation in our relationship that occurred many years ago.

***

When we were younger, we would sit at the kitchen table creating masterpieces with Play-Doh, being sure not to mix the colors…God forbid! (But when we did, we would swirl them all together and turn them into a psychedelic mess.)

Our Sunday mornings would consist of making imprints of the funny pages from the newspaper with Silly Putty and then stretching the faces of the characters into distortion until we laughed ourselves silly.

Hours were spent building Lincoln Log homes, only to destroy them like Godzilla.

We would carefully connect Hot Wheel tracks together through the house, propping some up with chairs to gain some height, creating a highway that ran from one end of the house to the other, and then raced cars down the track to see whose would travel furthest.

Growing up with two older brothers meant that I was introduced to playing football, softball, foursquare, fishing, wiffleball, basketball and whatever else the boys and their friends did. Luckily, we had a very large fenced-in backyard that was perfect for throwing a ball around and a large hill for sledding during the winter.

Our house was the "go-to" house that many of the kids in the subdivision came to for play. Not only did my mother take on babysitting jobs to supplement the household income, but kids from our subdivision and surrounding subdivisions seemed to be drawn to our house. I suppose that the parents of the kids who would come and spend the day playing felt secure that my mom would dutifully ensure that their children were taken care of, which she always did.

Who Will Save Me from Grandpa?

My brothers were never at a loss for friends and were extremely popular in school. Cal had graduated high school the year prior to me entering that realm. Craig and I were just a year apart in school and attended the same high school for two years. Countless times girls at school would approach me and ask, "Is Craig your brother? He is so cute! You don't look anything like him!"

My identity seemed to be "Craig's little sister" in school. Although I was very proud that Craig was my brother, as a little sister who was struggling with her own acceptance and self-image, hearing this common phrase only made me feel like more of a pariah.

I was lucky enough to have two friends in my neighborhood that I spent a lot of time with, both coincidentally named Tracy. Our imaginations kept us occupied while playing with Barbies, Legos, board games and other fun things, with plenty of giggling surrounding all of it. I was known to laugh so hard until I cried! We would climb trees, take hikes in the woods behind our houses, ride bikes, and truly had fun with each other.

In the days before all of the electronic gadgets that now leave kids glaring at a screen, we spent the day playing outside, sometimes well into the evening. We all knew to listen for our names being called out from the direction of our respective homes when the first hints of dusk began throwing shadows towards the darkness.

The rituals of making sure homework was done for the next school day and getting a bath to wash off the day's play before we settled down for a little television before bedtime were the norm. A kiss goodnight from Mom and Dad and then off to our bedrooms we would go. Once tucked into my bed, I felt comforted by the soft light streaming in from the living room and the muffled sounds of my parents watching television and talking about their days. I felt protected while I was home with my brothers and my parents. Outside the comforts of home, no one was aware of the heinous events that I was enduring.

Outwardly, I appeared as though I fit into my family. Internally, I was in constant turmoil from feeling like I was an unworthy, useless appendage that just needed amputation.

I didn't know it was supposed to be any other way.

Chapter 8 ~ The Ugly Duckling and the Black Sheep

All of my childhood memories I see through the eyes of a wounded little girl who carried a heaviness and sadness inside that never allowed me to truly be myself. Even though I remember laughing and having fun, it is the feelings of sadness that prevail.

***

I never felt I had enough athletic ability or self-esteem to be part of a sports team, so I passed every time my parents asked me if I was interested in joining a team. When I was ten years old I finally decided to join a softball team.

At my very first practice, as I eagerly stood in the field with my stiff new ball glove (that my dad and I so carefully shopped for) on my hand, one of the female coaches made the comment that I was a horrible softball player and that I was "too fat to play", within the earshot of everyone on the field.

I hadn't even been given a chance yet!

Other remarks by the coaches made it very clear there were girls on the team that had experience, and that they were highly favored over a newbie like me. That day I took another blow to my self-confidence, this time from adults.

I quit the team that day.

I told my parents I was never going back to play on that softball team because I was horrible player. They encouraged me that I would get better with practice. I told them of the demeaning words the coach had uttered about me. Of course, my parents didn't believe me at first, but after I assured them that she did, I never had to go back.

Any desire I had to become part of a team or to participate in sports was murdered that day, along with another piece of my psyche.

***

I was always very shy when I would meet new people or when I would try to make friends with other kids. I was an awkward, curly haired, buck toothed, chubby girl with very little self confidence. In the 1970s, I seemed to be poster-child for bullying. I think it was hard for

Mom to understand this because she has always been very confident. She tried to make me confident through her experiences.

Name calling, not being included in others' groups, feeling like I stuck out like a sore thumb waiting to have the hammer smack it again was the norm for me as long as I can remember. I expected to be criticized or humiliated by someone no matter where I was and who I was with; kids, teachers, or adults all had taken a poke at me at some time or another, so I was always on guard.

Many times I did suffer undue judgment. Even though I made an effort to conform to what was expected of me, I always felt as though I was doing *everything* wrong. I expected that others were judging my appearance, actions or opinions. I felt absolutely ugly. I liked nothing about myself and I didn't know why. I never tried to make sense of it, I just accepted that I was different and for some reason I was a bully magnet. Unfortunately, because I thought everybody hated me, I hated myself, too.

Sadly, I wasn't aware that kids are supposed to be carefree, have fun, and not be overwhelmed by feelings of inferiority and hideousness. I just assumed that these feelings of worthlessness and being a target for bullies were a normal part of growing up, along with repetitive sexual abuse.

I walked through life with extreme anxiety every moment of the day, waiting to be pounced on, which was debilitating for me.

The bullying and name calling, which usually came from boys, followed me through graduation from high school, along with low self-esteem that seemed to fuel the verbal bashing,

Neighborhood boys, boys in my classes, even boys that I had never met before, like the boys that went to the same school as I did or random boys at a shopping mall, seemed to think I was a target for their bullying. Everywhere I went I was victimized by verbal assaults, which usually had to do with my appearance. I was never one of the "cute girls", and I didn't belong to any clique. I had not created a negative reputation for myself, but for some reason I attracted much unwanted attention by quietly trying to fit in.

I rarely informed my parents of the hateful phrases and comments

Chapter 8 ~ The Ugly Duckling and the Black Sheep

that I endured on a daily basis. In one instance, I told my parents of the persistent verbal abuse I received from a boy that lived just a few houses down from ours. In my defense, my parents requested this boy's parents to come to our house to discuss how appallingly the boy had been treating me.

Once inside our kitchen, my dad addressed the boy's father regarding the demeaning situation, giving the example of the son calling me a "fat ass". This boy's father responded with, "Well, she is a fat ass, isn't she?"

I stood in utter disbelief that I had just heard these words exit this man's mouth. I looked at my stunned father with a disheartened, doe-eyed stare, which prompted Dad to order the insufferable man out of our home. I am sure that there was no way my dad could have anticipated this man's behavior because if he had, surely he would have protected me from it. It became obvious to us that the boy had learned his offensive way of treating others from his vile father. Dad reassured me that their actions were not acceptable and to disregard that any of it ever happened.

Feeling hopeless, I imagined most parents would react the same revolting way if approached and informed that their child was bullying another so I learned to keep a closed mouth about any further victimization that I was the recipient of.

***

When I was ten years old, my mother became pregnant again. At that time, we did not know the sex of the baby so I was hoping for a little sister since I already had two brothers.

On a warm summer day in 1976, my little brother, Corey, was born. I was excited but disappointed I didn't get the little sister I had hoped for.

Corey was a sweet natured little boy with a quirky sense of humor and a fondness of Star Wars toys. I can still describe him this way today except for the fact he is brilliant, like our dad.

I have watched Corey mature into a sweet natured man with a love for God and his family and is a blessing to all that cross his path.

In my early teen years, I realized I was bombarding my little brother with unfair and sometimes borderline abusive treatment instead of the love and guidance that is expected from a big sister. I had the tendency to be very short with him and I remember once pushing him down in his playpen when he was about two years old.

I had become the bully.

I felt such extreme guilt from that one despicable action that I knew I had to change my behavior and try to treat him like the special little boy that he was. I knew I could not cause anyone else the pain that I had already endured in my short life.

Corey will forever hold that certain "soft spot" in my heart that I created for him after this.

***

As years went by, I found myself internalizing all of this pain and hate and grief, which resulted in severe depression and I became very self-destructive. My mind was consumed with constant consideration of suicide and the method that would serve me best.

I would brutally punch my legs until they were black and blue to punish myself. I would hold my breath in an internal scream until blood vessels would break in my face. I felt I did not matter to anyone and I had no valid purpose in this horrible life and no one would miss me.

During my high school years it became a necessity for me to protect myself. The anger and humiliation that swelled from years of verbal torment finally emerged as violent outbursts that involved physical attacks on the perpetrators. I found that one blow, or even just a threat to cause physical harm to these abusive boys, was enough to make them stop their hateful words and actions towards me. It became my new reaction to the bullying.

In the middle of a college prep English class, my tolerance of the verbal abuse I had taken for several years resulted in an explosive

Chapter 8 ~ The Ugly Duckling and the Black Sheep

reaction. He whispered something hateful to me, and without thinking, I stood up and landed a hard punch on his chest. I knocked the very breath out of him. As he sat gasping, I glared at him and sat back down at my desk. Fortunately, the teacher did not see me punch him and no one around our desks said a word. From then on, he spoke to me with kindness.

There was a boy I met in my sophomore year of high school. We were in a couple classes together and he took a liking to me, which I reciprocated. After several months of "liking" each other, something changed and his phone calls and affections ended and he became hateful to me. He would call me names, say horrible things to me, and eventually I had endured enough. As one of the classes we had together ended, the bell rang and I followed him out of the classroom and into the hallway. I reached up, grabbed his curly, blonde hair and pulled his six-foot-plus frame down to the floor. While multitudes of kids were walking around his body as I stood over him, I looked him square in the face and said, "Don't you EVER bother me again!"

He responded with a string of profanities, but he never bothered me again.

There were many neighborhood kids, along with kids who rode the same school bus as I did, who would bully me. After tolerating a long period of being belittled by a neighborhood boy, we stepped off of the bus after school. I proceeded to trip him with one foot and shove his body onto the asphalt road. With an intimidating voice, I demanded that he never speak to me again. He never did.

I had ignored a group of seven high school boys who followed me in the halls for two weeks straight during my junior year. They would chant, yes...*chant*, disparaging comments about me while walking behind me. My plan was to continue ignoring them but one had the nerve to grab me from behind with one arm and place his hand from his other arm over my mouth. Much to their surprise, I quickly turned around in my captor's arms, grabbed his shirt collar in my tightly balled up fist and slammed him up against some lockers, rattling them with the force.

While I held his fearful body against the lockers, the remaining six boys in the group stood with their mouths gaped open in shock while they watched the demise of their cohort.

With clenched teeth and with as much intimidation that I could muster, I compellingly advised my assailant, "Don't you ever bother me again!"

None of them did.

Although it took me years to stand up for myself against the ceaseless bullying from my peers, the years I was attacked with the damaging words that others said to me had taken its toll. There were many boys and girls who used me as a verbal punching bag with their derogatory words for as long as I could remember. Any shred of self-confidence that I should have developed was non-existent.

I found that it did not take self-confidence to defend myself; I was simply practicing a basic survival technique.

Chapter Nine

Standing in Shadows

"Laundry Day"

It is an overcast summer morning. Under the cover of the large screened-in porch at my grandparents' house, I am sitting on the white painted rocking chair that is part of their patio furniture set. All of the chairs have vinyl chair cushions printed with green, orange and yellow flowers. While I am forcefully rocking with exaggerated body movements, I am considering what I will do with my day. Since I don't see sunlight falling over the edges of the roof, I would not be going to the lake to swim any time soon.

Outside of the main entry into my grandparents' house is a heavy, brown wooden door, situated at a right angle to the main door. Behind this door is a narrow, closet-like room which houses a clothes washer and dryer, a makeshift rope clothesline with coats on metal hangers dangling from it and is lined with shelves. These shelves have varying sizes of cardboard boxes on them that hold mysterious items, except for the box on the top shelf on the far wall. Unfortunately, the contents of this box are known: pornographic magazines that my grandfather has previously introduced me to. The room has a very distinctive odor of laundry detergent and old cardboard. The room is dimly illuminated by a single light bulb, haphazardly hanging from the center of the ceiling, and requires a pull chain to turn it on and off.

I glance over the sea of green indoor-outdoor carpeting and I notice my grandfather has started doing the laundry.

The laundry room door is open and my grandfather has sorted his and my grandmother's garments and I hear the whirring of the washer.

I decide to go indoors and find something to do or maybe watch television. I walk by the open door, and I am unexpectedly solicited to go into the laundry room with my grandfather. I assume he needs me to help with the task of doing laundry, or he wants to show me something. This is not a place I have been inappropriately lured to before, so I can only assume that his intentions were pure in his request. Being the

Who Will Save Me from Grandpa?

dutiful granddaughter that I am expected to be when I am there visiting, I indulge him and enter the small, shadowy room with him.

He assists me up to sit on top of the washer and proceeds with his assault.

Just inside the house, approximately 10 feet away, I know my grandmother is sitting in her recliner. Just like all of the other times, she remains conveniently unaware of this repulsion, as I agonize over the possibility of being caught.

Still focused on the chilly feel of the washer underneath me, the whir of the machine and the unique scent of the room, I pacify myself with the familiarity of this type of affair; the reassurance that as soon as that clichéd handkerchief is brought out of his pocket this violation is soon to be over and I can go back to being a kid again.

Due to my intense fear of being judged and criticized, I was painfully anxious of being put in new situations. The first day of school was usually dreadful for me. My heart would pound out of my chest as the day neared. I learned to absolutely hate beginning a new school year because of the debilitating anxiety I would feel. That feeling never changed throughout all of my years of school and even into college. Although, the feeling waned with each new semester of college, the anxiety was still as intense when I would start a new job.

Simple undertakings, such as reading out loud or singing in front of anyone, including my family, would paralyze me with fear of making a mistake or facing judgment. I dreaded when a teacher would seek out a student in class to read a passage aloud. As the teacher would scan the students for a willing participant I would sink down in my desk chair, hoping to not be noticed. Much to my demise, cowering in my seat did not make me invisible and I would have to face my fear and read aloud occasionally. In addition to blood rushing into my face and my heart pounding out of my chest, embarrassment would overcome me. I would stammer through the words I was reading while the discriminating eyes of my peers seemed to burn through my very soul.

I have a love for singing and I sang in choirs from elementary school into my freshman year of high school. I was chosen to be in our school's elite choir in my freshman year, but I was petrified to sing solo in front of anyone, which was a requirement in order to be graded and placed accordingly within the choir. A lot of the music we were taught to sing was chamber music, so the instructor would call us to the front of the room in groups so all of the parts could be heard together. This was my only saving grace, since I didn't have to stand up there alone. Meekly, I sang my alto-1 part of whatever song was chosen for us. Somehow, I pulled it off.

I chose not to participate in any other choirs past my freshman year due to the painful anxiety I felt about performing a solo performance. Looking back, I feel that I missed out on something I really enjoyed, plus the chance to develop my voice.

I spent the rest of my high school years not being involved in anything due to the debilitating fear of judgment. I remained withdrawn, and in turn, failed to take advantage of many experiences. I avoided any and all dances, proms, team sports and just about every other social event in high school.

I faked my way through being a teenager. I purposely missed out on many pivotal events. I would suffer through and do as little as I could to get by in school. My grades suffered, my relationships suffered and all of this just reinforced my belief that I was a worthless, unviable part of a cruel life.

***

Despite living with the negative effects that were forced upon me, I have always had a goofy, quick witted, sarcastic sense of humor. My two older brothers, as well as their friends, taught me to find humor in crude and distasteful "boyish" things. Other kids enjoyed my sense of humor, too. It was the one characteristic that allowed me to make a few friends.

While my friends were on sports teams, going to parties and dating, I lived my life at the periphery. Turned so inward, I became somewhat invisible to others, and as a result I was left off of lists for social invitations and remained invisible to boys. Formal dances, prom, and graduation parties all went on without me.

Fortunately, I was blessed with my cousin, Deanna. While some of my other friends were taking part in typical teenager activities, I spent time with her. Since she was three years younger than me, her schedule was not bogged down with customary "teenager stuff".

Deanna and I became more like sisters than cousins. We were always together, sharing our special brand of silliness and laughter.

Chapter Ten

The Promise

"Relaxing on the Couch"

I am walking through my grandparents' small living room. This room is sparsely furnished with, a brown, wooden rocking chair, a brown vinyl recliner where my grandmother spends most of her time, and a long, light green upholstered couch that they call the "davenport". There is also a television set and a few end tables with lamps atop them.

My grandfather stops me and asks me to sit on the arm of the davenport. The arms of this couch sharply tilt inward, so it is not a comfortable place to sit. He begins his immoral mistreatment of me.

My grandmother is just in the next room. I lay there, overflowing with fear that she will get in her wheelchair, come out of her bedroom and find us. I stare at the ceiling, waiting for him to remove his crushing weight off of my body and hope we remain unseen.

The vile handkerchief comes out of his pocket, and as always, we go about our day as "normal".

Almost a year had gone by since I had been told that I "could have stopped it at any time". I had never told anyone about the atrocities that I had experienced. In my mind, it was over. What I carried with me was an enormous amount of guilt, confusion, and sincere hope that no one else would ever have to endure what I did.

Throughout the years of the abuse, I struggled to make sense of what was happening to me. Since it began when I was a toddler, having my grandfather "love" me seemed normal.

As I grew older and began to have ideas that my grandfather's behavior was not appropriate, I continued to submit to his requests because I was expected to be obedient, caring and loving to my family, especially to elders. When my parents would leave me in my grandparents' care it came with a stern reminder to listen "do what I was told" and to behave, which is exactly what I did.

Into my preteen years, I began having stronger feelings that the things my grandfather coerced me to participate in were wrong. As I progressed through phases of believing that his behavior was normal when I was younger, and then questioning his behavior as I was becoming a young woman, was extremely difficult. As adolescence and puberty set in, I was struggling with hormonal changes and all of the complicated events that are all part of growing up, along with the added obstacle of what he was doing to my body and mind.

Once I had found the inner strength to end the abuse and tell him to stop doing these sinful things to me, I tried not to think about the ten years that had been "different" for me. Being a teenager was difficult enough without the additional burdens that I was left to carry.

Within a year after I ended the abuse, I stumbled across an edition of *The Reader's Digest* that was sitting on top of the toilet tank in the half-bath just off the family room in our split-foyer home. On the front cover the words "incest" and "taboo" glared at me. I did not know what the word "incest" meant but I knew what "taboo" meant, so that intrigued me. Thinking my parents would possibly prohibit me from reading the article because of the word "taboo", I felt somewhat devious and picked up the magazine and read it anyway. Much to my surprise, it was an article written about children being sexually abused by family members!

I had no idea that these unspeakable acts of immorality had been inflicted on others! As I held this epiphany in black and white in my fourteen-year-old hands, I was shocked, sickened and relieved at the same time that there was a name for the atrocity!

Now armed with this new information, I resolved to keep my secret locked deep within myself with the belief that *it was over.*

No one would believe me anyway and if I said anything I am sure I would be punished.
What if I caused it to happen?
I must have done something to deserve this.
What would it hurt by keeping it a secret?

Chapter 10 ~ The Promise

Soon after I read the revealing article that undoubtedly became a pinnacle in my life, my conscious attempt at burying this wickedness came to an abrupt halt.

On a Monday, the parochial school Deanna attended had the day off for a holiday. My mom had been asked to babysit my then eleven-year-old cousin and her little sister, which was something she did not routinely do.

When I came home from school that day, I found Deanna waiting to play with my Barbie Dolls with me.

We sat on my bedroom floor and played with my dolls, dressing Barbie and her friends in funky, brightly colored 1970s style bellbottom jumpsuits and white go-go boots. Even though I was a freshman in high school, I found it perfectly normal to still occasionally play with Barbie dolls, especially when Deanna wanted to play.

As we sat on my dark green shag carpeted floor with heaps of handmade doll clothes scattered around us, Deanna interrupted our play by saying, "I have something to tell you but I can't say it out loud."

I was alarmed by these words. I knew Deanna to be quite the chatterbox and she was not one to hold back if she had something to say. She said she would write it down for me. I scrambled for the nearest piece of paper I could find; a brown paper grocery sack. I promptly slid it in front of her as she was seated on the floor. I hovered concernedly over her as she wrote the words.

I saw the gut-wrenching words *"Grandpa is a pervert"* in eleven-year-old scrawl screaming from the surface of the drab paper sack.

I suddenly felt my chest tighten and my stomach turn.

Oh, my God! It had happened to her!

The years of hoping no one else would ever have to suffer such perversion by our grandfather was immediately obliterated.

I knew then that my silence had to end.

As Deanna and I sat cross-legged on the carpet facing each other, we talked about things that no eleven-year-old and fourteen-year-old children should ever have to experience, speak about, think about or even know about. We did not discuss specific events. I assured her that she was not alone, that I had experienced the same things she had. We

~ 41 ~

Who Will Save Me from Grandpa?

agreed that our primary objective should be to tell our parents about what had happened to us to help protect the younger children in the family. A sincere promise was made between us to do just that…first chance we had.

I don't know why we didn't run to my mom and expel this urgent information right then. Instead, we spent the rest of the late afternoon into the evening continuing to play with my Barbie dolls.

My aunt arrived after her day at work to collect Deanna and her sister to take them home. I went about the rest of my evening as normal, except I fought with myself in my fourteen-year-old mind just how I should approach this situation.

I decided to stay silent, regardless of the promise I made to Deanna. Guilt and shame and the possibility of judgment and punishment reigned over the pact that we made.

***

Two days later, on Wednesday at 8:30 pm, I was already tucked into bed. On school nights, I went to bed early so I could get up at 4:30 am. This allowed ample time to take a shower, blow dry my coarse, curly hair straight and then use a curling iron to style my hair so that I fit in with the rest of the girls in ninth grade. I would then meticulously apply make-up to accentuate the one thing that I believed was attractive about me; my eyes.

I liked being in my bedroom. I enjoyed rearranging my furniture to accommodate me and my goldfish and hamster roommates.

My room was comforting to me, with its buttery yellow walls that were covered with posters of Shaun Cassidy, Scott Baio and other pictures of cute boys that glossed the covers of *Tiger Beat* magazine. My twin bed was centered on one wall of my small, square bedroom. My antiqued white desk that Dad hand crafted to match my hand-carved, antique dresser were positioned on each side of the headboard, which left little room for much else.

My attempt to fall asleep was abruptly interrupted by my mom frantically throwing open my bedroom door. She had been at a

Chapter 10 ~ The Promise

meeting with my uncle, Deanna's dad, which they would attend every Wednesday evening.

She flipped the light switch to turn the overhead light on in my room.

With a distraught look on her face and in a wavering voice she asked, "Do you have something to tell me about one of our family members?"

I became aware in that moment that Deanna had spilled the beans to her folks, so the time for me to come clean about the molestation now presented itself; thwarting my decision to bury our secret and the promise to Deanna that I had made.

Overwhelmed with concern, my mom sat down gently on my bed next to me and I proceeded to succinctly tell her that grandpa had been molesting me. I can only imagine how hearing these words crushed my mom's soul.

She wrapped her arms around me as we wept together. After purging this information, although brief and nondescript, I felt as though a great weight had been lifted from me. I felt a rush of freedom and relief wash over me that I had finally, after all of these years, shared my secret.

I never told Mom specifics or graphic details of the ten years of abuse that had been inflicted upon me by her father, but telling her this secret made scattered pieces of this deranged puzzle fit together for her. The physical evidence that presented itself over the years and my behavioral clues began to make sense now. She felt extreme guilt. She kept repeating, "I should have known! I should have seen the signs!"

After the initial shock of this despicable revelation, my mom's attempt at rationalizing the situation set in.

She then said something that will resonate with me until the end of time.

I understand why she said it.

I understand she was trying to make sense out of this appalling information that she was just force-fed for her to deal with.

In a matter-of-fact way, my mom then said, "Well, you know grandma has been in a wheelchair for a long time."

~ 43 ~

Who Will Save Me from Grandpa?

Did she just say what I THINK she said?

Her words absolutely dumbfounded me. I tried to make sense out of what she had just said.

In my mind, making an excuse for her father's wicked behavior was giving him permission to perform his vile acts on children.

The precedence of the way the abuse was handled from then on was set in that moment.

We did not matter.

I carried her piercing words in the deepest part of my being from then on.

We then spoke of the very real concern regarding the younger children in the family. My little brother, Corey, was only four years old at the time, along with two younger girl cousins and another on the way. Mom told me the plan the adults in the family would now follow was to keenly supervise any children while around my grandfather so he would not have a chance to be alone with any of them to repeat his crime. That idea satisfied me at the time.

Mom told me to try and get some sleep and left me. Relief that I finally had shared my devastating secret, relief that the younger children in our family would now be protected from the monster that had ravaged me and my cousin and complete emotional exhaustion sent me fast to sleep.

The following morning, Dad walked into my room as I was getting ready for school. His face showed weariness, as if he had not slept through the night.

With tears streaming down his tired face, he said, "If I could lock you up behind iron bars so no one could hurt you I would. But I can't."

My dad mentioning locking me behind iron bars instead of my offender was a bit ironic and saddened me. I know he meant it in a protective way, but I had already been living in a prison of sorts for years with a never-ending sentence, while the person that created that prison remained free.

Dad was not present in my room when I revealed the abuse to my mother. She informed him of the events after she had left my room for me to go to sleep. I know they were both devastated. After this

Chapter 10 ~ The Promise

revelation, the focus that should have been on my well-being never materialized.

I was left to live as I had been; struggling with becoming a young adult with all this extra baggage to deal with.

***

It turns out, Deanna had gone to school the following day after we made our promise to each other and told one of the instructors at school about the abuse. The information made it back to her parents via several others in the process.

She had kept her promise.

In retrospect, I am not sure I would have ever disclosed the information without Deanna's intervention. I can only imagine what my life would be like had that been the case, as I now understand the incredibly negative impact that the abuse has had on my mental and physical health.

Revealing our "little secret" was the first glimmer of the hope of healing from the effects of the malevolence Deanna and I suffered.

I sincerely thank you, Deanna.

Chapter Eleven
A Dark New Day

"Morning Coffee"

The morning sun is streaming through the open curtains and warming the living room as I exit the bedroom where I sleep in when I stay with my grandparents. The television is on, indicating that my grandfather is awake and watching the morning news.

I walk into the kitchen side of the aluminum edged, yellow Formica peninsula and sit on the chair to the right of him.

He pours me a cup of coffee, which is something that only my grandpa would let me drink at such a young age. Most kids do not get to drink coffee, but I was allowed to drink it when I was at my grandparent's house. It was sort of "our little secret".

I heavily add sugar and creamer, and sip on my sweet and creamy caffeine laden secret treat.

My grandfather asks me to touch him in a vulgar manner, which I do because I was told to mind my grandparents while I am at their house. My obedience initiates another episode of sexual abuse by my grandfather and finishes with his well-worn handkerchief. Again, my grandmother is just in the next room, and somehow again, we aren't discovered.

After revealing our secret to our parents and witnessing their reactions and hearing their feelings on the matter, we did gain some relief from exposing what had happened to us. But that was all. As far as we knew, the matter was in our parents' hands now and we could go about being our young selves.

As time passed, it seemed as if our parents' concern regarding the impact of the sexual abuse and its effects evaporated. The subject was never brought up for discussion and counseling was never offered.

Chapter 11 ~ A Dark New Day

Ultimately, we were left to fend for ourselves to process the rape of our bodies, minds and souls.

***

Years after the truth was exposed, I asked my mom if there had been any steps taken to penalize my grandfather for his crimes. She explained to me that punishment for a man who had emphysema and had a couple of strokes was futile. They figured he didn't have long to live, anyway, but she did tell me that they informed him that the family knew that he had sexually abused us.

All I could think was that the strokes he suffered did not impede his attempt at molesting me on the day that I finally ended his reign over my body.

Hell, I watched the man get struck by lightning one summer while he was retrieving minnow traps from a stream during a severe thunderstorm! Even that "sign" didn't stop him from sexually abusing me!

When I questioned my mom if they were going to enlighten my grandmother that her husband molested her granddaughters, her response was, "We can't do that! That would *kill* her!"

Our parents' approach at rectifying the theft of our childhood, our innocence, and the physical and mental affects still to be revealed to us was unacceptable to me.

Feelings of absolute worthlessness, having suicidal thoughts, severe anxiety and depression, promiscuity, the inability to have healthy relationships with others and PTSD were all the product of suffering the abuse at my grandfather's hands.

There was no New Day for us, but only dark days ahead.

Chapter Twelve
Rest in Pieces

On a November morning in 1981, prior to my alarm alerting me to wake up and get ready for school, Mom entered my bedroom and gently woke me. Her face was sorrowful and her voice was shaky when she informed me that my grandfather had passed away overnight after spending several days in the hospital suffering from emphysema and other medical conditions.

She then explained to me that a pastor my parents knew had come to the hospital to offer my grandfather peace and comfort in his final hours on earth. As the pastor spoke to my grandfather, apparently he offered the Word of Salvation through Jesus Christ to my grandfather. My mother said that he accepted Jesus Christ as his Savior on his death bed, and that he was forgiven for his sins and is now in Heaven. After lovingly patting me on the arm, she left my bedroom.

I felt no sorrow. I felt nothing but relief.

With my belief in Salvation through Jesus Christ, I believe that my grandfather is in Heaven, although I still struggle with the notion. I believe my God is a forgiving God and that He has mercy on all souls, not denying Salvation and entrance into the Kingdom of Heaven for someone who committed such atrocious acts as my grandfather did. It is a difficult idea to fathom, but as a fifteen-year-old, I put trust in what my mother had said and left it at that.

The day of the funeral, Deanna and I were puzzled at why my mom and her brothers were so distraught and tearful at the passing of this monster.

We shed no tears. We were gleeful in the fact that he was dead.

My grandfather had passed away approximately a year and a half after the reveal of his crime against his granddaughters. The only justice that was served was the fact that he was dead and that he could not hurt anybody else. My mother was now four months pregnant and I

Chapter 12 ~ Rest in Pieces

was ever-so-grateful that this new sibling of mine would never know this wretched man.

His legacy was two shattered young girls who, unbeknownst to them, had the fight of their lives ahead of them.

***

On an early morning in March of 1982, my beautiful little sister, Courtnie, was brought into this world.

I was ecstatic that I finally had a little sister! I loved my brothers and they all held a special part of my heart, but I had always felt I was missing a piece of my soul that none of them could fill. I knew the moment I gazed upon the chubby-cheeked sweetness that was my new baby sister that my world was now somehow better.

Courtnie was a bright, extremely witty, adorable and talented little girl and was the absolute light of my life. The almost sixteen years in age difference between us never really made a difference to us, although, I was flattered to be mistaken for her mother more than once!

The unbreakable connection I was blessed to have with her soul is one I yearned for as a child but was gifted to me just when I needed it most.

Her existence brightened the darkness I lived in.

Chapter Thirteen

Into the Pit

In high school, my feelings of inferiority and worthlessness inhibited me from participating in extracurricular activities. Instead, I would go home and sleep.

Sleep was my drug of choice, providing me with an escape full of dreams. I have always had vivid dreams and I possess the ability to remember them in great detail. I would have many recurring dreams. One featured a talking spider that sat on a bar of soap on the ledge of a sink in very old, dim log cabin. The cabin smelled like boiling pinto beans and had been used as slave quarters prior to the Civil War. In another dream, my brothers and I would be playing Cowboys and Indians. Real "Indians" would appear, riding motorcycles and would shoot arrows at us kids as we played on our next-door neighbors' jungle-gym. Fortunately, in this dream, I had a magic bean that I swallowed that was designed to instantly grow an arrow out of my chest that made me appear already impaled and dead so the savages would leave me alone. Another involved an evil witch who chased me with a bloody severed arm through dark underground tunnels. Due to these strange tales that would take hold of my mind during slumber, they were quite entertaining and created an escape for me.

Many times, I would have nightmares that I couldn't fully wake up from. I would scream with all of my might but no sound would come out. I felt I was aware of my surroundings while I lay in my bed in a semi-conscious state; terrified, trapped and helpless, emitting a silent scream.

One Saturday morning I awoke with tears streaming down my face. I had dreamt that my brothers and I were playing basketball on our driveway. While standing on the concrete slab driveway as my brothers dribbled the ball around me, I looked up towards my bedroom window and there stood my deceased grandfather, glaring at me from inside my bedroom. This dream distressed me greatly, and I felt I should mention the way I was feeling to my mom.

Still weeping from the impact of the dream, I walked across the hall and into her bedroom. I sat down on her bed and started telling her about my dream.

We discussed it briefly until my dad walked in. He questioned why I was so upset and then we brought him up to speed about the situation. Since Dad is forever a problem solver, he went into action.

As he leaned against a chest of drawers in their room, he began to counsel me. He advised me that the resolution for my discomfort was for me to envision digging a hole in the deepest part of my mind, bury all of the dreadful experiences and memories in that hole and cover it up and go on with life.

I knew my Dad was a brilliant man and I assumed that his solution had merit. I walked back into my bedroom and sat on my bed. I began imagining digging a deep, dark pit way in the back of my mind. I dumped boxes and boxes of the horrible memories into the gaping hole and then covered it up to be disregarded.

Chapter Fourteen
Easy Prey

I took a job at a popular fast food restaurant while I was in high school. Before the automation of fast food, the grill area was a non-stop kitchen that needed proficient workers to keep up the fast pace.

After a short time working there, I was approached by one of the managers. He told me that I was a good candidate for a career as a manager for this restaurant chain. I briefly considered this option for my future but I did not have enough confidence in myself to move forward with that venture.

What no one seemed to see was the crippling anxiety that I had in any situation. I existed in a constant state of fear that I was doing something terribly wrong. That fear and anxiety was the fuel that seemed to drive me to become somewhat of a master in my work at the restaurant. It seemed that the only way I could find minimal comfort and a little peace was by gaining acceptance from my peers by demonstrating hard work and mastering a skill. With that method of influencing people, I hoped it would appear that I was self-confident regardless of the violent storm that was raging inside of me. Unfortunately, sometimes this façade of self-confidence was read by others as arrogance.

I became a very good actress in regards to fooling others that I had it together. Inside was a much damaged little girl who was always on a heightened state of alert, vigilantly waiting for the next person who wanted to hurt me.

***

In my junior year of high school, I became friends with a guy named Jim in my art class. He then introduced me to a group of his friends and his girlfriend, Kelly. My new friends all lived further south and didn't go to our school.

My new friend, Charlie, would pick me up in his awesome

Chapter 14 ~ Easy Prey

1970-something Chevy Malibu and we would ride in his coconut scented interior to Kelly's house. We would play games, hang out and usually find a burger joint to eat at.

During one visit, while Charlie was having his hair cut on the porch by Kelly's mom, I sat at the kitchen table by myself. Kelly's father came up behind me and started touching my shoulders and then started moving his hands down onto my breasts. I froze. I could not believe he was doing this to me! With panic surging through my body, Charlie walked back into the kitchen and my violator quickly removed his hands from me. I wanted to leave right then but I knew my friends had other plans, so I reluctantly stayed.

Later on, while Charlie and I traveled back to my house, I told him what Kelly's father had done to me.

"Bad things happen to everyone", he responded.

I felt like I was destined to be prey.

We rode the rest of the way home in silence.

Chapter Fifteen

Positively Negative

I had an interest in the dental field after going through orthodontic therapy in my teens. When it came time to consider what career I would pursue, I researched the different aspects of the dental field and determined that I would enroll in the dental assisting program at a local community college. This program was two semesters long, which was the amount of time I was willing to spend in college. My experience in high school was so painful for me, and I had no reason to assume college would be any different. Two semesters was all I could afford since I was paying for my tuition, books and supplies with my savings from my part time job at the restaurant. I had also convinced myself that I wasn't smart enough to obtain a degree in dental hygiene.

I found that college was much different than high school and I excelled! I had found my niche and I loved everything about it. Soon after graduating with excellent grades, earning the degree of Certificate of Proficiency in Dental Assisting and passing the Dental Assisting National Board Exam, I was a Certified Dental Assistant.

I was hired as a chairside assistant at a dental office near where I lived with my parents. I did not have my own car so I relied on my mom to drive me to work if she needed the car for the day. Otherwise, I would borrow her car and drive myself. I purposely accepted this position due to these factors.

The dentist I assisted for was technically a very good dentist but an appalling employer. He played on my good nature and my lack of self-confidence. I allowed him to throw bloody, saliva soaked cotton at my face, aggressively toss blood caked instruments at me and verbally abuse me. I would be in tears on a daily basis. Getting out of bed to go to a place where I was abused made me very anxious and even more

Chapter 15 ~ Positively Negative

depressed. Once I brought this fact up to my father, his advice was to "stick it out". So I did. I tolerated this abuse for a year and a half.

***

There was one person in my life who offered me something that no one else seemed to be able to; complete and unconditional acceptance, understanding and support in any endeavor I chose to embark upon. This person was my dad's mom, Kay Williams. I referred to her as my "good grandma" and my "fun" grandma.

I was fortunate to frequently spend time with her. She was full of love and full of life. I never felt anxious or out of place with her and she accepted me for my pure soul and nothing else. She thought I was beautiful and around her I felt beautiful.

She was forever demonstrative with hugs, kisses and compliments. She had a love for animals with the same passion that I have always had.

Once I had chosen to go to college for dental assisting, I found out then that she was a dental assistant in the 1940s! Dentistry was far different than it is today, but it was just one more thing she and I had in common. I was so very fortunate to have someone with their soul in sync with mine.

Just a few days before my Sweet Grandma passed away unexpectedly, she and I spoke on the phone. I told her that I had an interest in going back to college to earn my degree in dental laboratory technology, which she enthusiastically encouraged me to do. Once she passed away, I knew I needed to fulfill that interest. It was literally the last thing she and I spoke about, so I wanted to earn that degree in memory of her.

***

Prior to enrolling in college for dental laboratory technology, I sought out dental lab tech positions in the classified want ads in the newspaper. I found a position at an orthodontic lab where the owner was willing to train me on my own time and with no pay. I would go there and train during the days I was off from the dental office I was working at with the abusive dentist.

However, my employer found out about my "side job" and abruptly terminated me. I didn't understand why he saw that as a problem, but then he told me that I was "too moody".

How could I not be moody when he was abusive and I was just there "sticking it out"?

I accepted my termination as a blessing since it offered me a way out of his hellish workplace. I worried that I might find another position where I would be victim to the same kind of abuse, so I made an oath to myself that I would not allow that to happen again, regardless what my dad recommended.

The position at the orthodontic lab never materialized due to the owner's poor health and he needed to close his lab.

After a long search, I found a position in a dental office in a neighborhood near the city. It was a changing neighborhood in the late 1980s with many long time residents and business owners moving away from the area due to blight and crime.

This new position as a dental assistant was a culture shock for me. I had never been exposed to a low-income neighborhood. Because of the location, this practice catered mostly to patients that had Medicaid. The patients were the working poor, the very poor, refugees and basically anyone who couldn't afford dental care. I loved knowing I was helping people that truly needed access to quality dental care.

Shorty after I started working full time in this dental practice, I became serious about going back to college and earning my Dental Laboratory Technology degree. I performed the necessary research, and I enrolled a dental lab tech program at the local community college.

I enjoyed college. I did not feel the judgment of my peers as strongly as I did in high school, and only I was held responsible for the outcome of my education. My parents discouraged me and my siblings from borrowing money for college. They could not afford to pay for it, so if we wanted a college education, we paid our own way.

The program required attendance from 8 am to 5 pm, five days a week. Our small group of fifteen or so students spent most of our time together. Relationships were developed; some friendly and some not.

I was 21 years old. I was working part time at the dental office,

Chapter 15 ~ Positively Negative

part-time at the fast food restaurant, and was attending college full-time. I was struggling with balancing many things, but mostly depression.

I began frequently drinking alcohol, becoming intoxicated in social settings and sometimes alone. I started not showing up for class, and if I did, I showed up late and drunk. I would sit in my car in the college parking lot and chug bottle after bottle of wine coolers prior to going to class.

This behavior snowballed into further self-deprecation and guilt. My mantra was of my incessant desire to die and I started frequently verbalizing this to some of my closer friends in class.

"I'd be better off dead. No one cares about me, anyway. No one would miss me. I just want to die!"

There was a bully in my class. I thought that I left that behind me in high school, but he was the exception. He would constantly call me hateful names and make inappropriate comments to me, usually about how I looked.

On a day I had come to class late and my mind was already in a dark place, several of us students were standing in the laboratory when he began to harass me.

I had tolerated enough of his antics. I began screaming at him at the top of my lungs. I was red-faced and violent, and I wanted to tear into him when several friends intervened to calm the rapidly escalating situation by restraining me by my arms and then pulled me out of the lab. They then attempted to coerce me into going to the counselor's office at the college for some help.

They could not watch me self-destruct any longer.

I firmly resisted and started running to the parking lot where my car was parked. They caught up with me, grabbed me again then physically dragged me to the counseling center.

As I sat in the counselor's office, I heard deep concern from my friends regarding my welfare. They felt they needed to do something... anything...to mediate. They were concerned by my constant threats of suicide.

Hearing my friends' concern and some well-placed words from the counselor, I came to the realization that I undeniably needed to seek professional psychiatric care. Prior to leaving, I promised them that I would find some help and I thanked them for their care and intervention.

That evening, I went home, sat Mom down at the kitchen table and told her that I wanted to die. I told her of my constant thoughts of suicide and that I had felt this way for a very long time. I told her of the intervention that my classmates had done because of their sincere worry about me.

Mom was horrified. She was finally seeing the pain that I had been living with for nearly two decades. The thought of her little girl taking a bunch of pills to off herself or putting a noose around her neck snapped my mom out of her 1950s idealism. She was calling a psychiatrist first thing in the morning.

***

The psychiatrist diagnosed me with major depression, prescribed me an antidepressant and appointed me with one of the psychologists in the office. The antidepressant I was prescribed was a very new drug at the time and little was known about its affects outside of the drug trials that were done with it. The drug was so new that it had not been published in drug reference publications yet.

Once I started taking the antidepressant, my mood became more predictable…it became predictably non-existent. The medication numbed any emotion I had. I could not cry. I was not able to become angry. My inhibitions vanished. I had become an emotionless zombie.

But, in my tranced state, I still had the desire to be loved.

Maintaining my chastity had always been very important to me. I vowed at a very young age to be a "good girl" and to wait to have sex when I married. (I never considered that my grandfather had already stolen that from me.)

Eventually, my intense desire to be loved was more important than chastity and I was willing to try whatever I needed to in an effort to find it.

I confused sex with love.

Chapter 15 ~ Positively Negative

I met a guy in a parking lot while driving around with Deanna one night. My folks weren't home that weekend, so I invited him and his friend to come back to my house. I proceeded to take this guy to my bedroom, and lost my "perceived" virginity. He left with his friend early in the morning and I never heard from him again. I went from feeling on top of the world, thinking that I found someone that cared about me. As the days went by, I realized that he was never going to call me and I felt increasing shame and loneliness.

Progressively, my promiscuity became more dangerous. I would go home with men that I just met to have sex with them, sometimes with no ride back to my car. I would go for rides with guys I just met and we would end up having sex in the car. I would have sex with men I met at parties. I would meet a man at a bar and then have sex in the parking lot. I would meet guys who still lived with their parents and we would have to sneak in so we could have sex.

One time I had gone for a ride with a guy I met at a small party. He drove me to a place that I was not familiar with, which somewhat concerned me. We began kissing. Next thing I knew, his pants were undone and he forcefully shoved my head towards his penis. I physically resisted him and somehow convinced him to take me back to my car, which he reluctantly did. That encounter scared me, but didn't stop me from placing myself into further risky situations.

In every example, these men cared nothing about me. I never heard from any of them after I allowed them to have sex with me.

All of the encounters where I was briefly enamored and willing to do whatever I needed to be loved, I put myself at risk for disease, pregnancy, rape, violence or even murder.

But, each time I allowed these men control over me only deepened the hell I was in.

Chapter Sixteen

Help or Hindrance?

My experience with the psychologist that I was appointed with never delved into the sexual abuse and how it affected me. She was the type of therapist who used the "blame everything on your mother" approach. When I realized that the nonsense that she was feeding me wasn't benefiting me in any way, I stopped seeing her.

I continued taking the antidepressant because the psychiatrist who prescribed it for me seemed to think it was helping.

After a while, I began to run a constant fever, felt very flu-like for weeks and my urine was the color of cola. Blood was taken and a hepatitis panel was done. Since I worked in the healthcare field, my physician suspected I had contracted the Hepatitis B virus from an infected patient. Fortunately, the panel came back negative, but I had absolutely suffered liver damage. It was determined to be a result of the antidepressant.

My doctor ordered me to stop taking it right away, but the psychiatrist I was seeing told me to keep taking it; he thought the benefits of the medication outweighed the side effects.

I had never been so ill in my life so I chose to listen to my physician and discontinued the drug. After some time, the symptoms from the liver damage from the drug decreased, but I was left with the symptoms of untreated depression and anxiety to still contend with.

Years went by as I continued to struggle with depression. Although I still contemplated suicide, I had become too apathetic, like I had lost the will to live.

I sought professional mental health care many times, and it seemed as all of the therapists I encountered had a wacky idea how to get to the root of my depression. The so called "treatment" was never healing in nature, and I never stayed with a therapist more than a short time due to their strange approaches. I decided that all psychological help was a

Chapter 16 ~ Help or Hindrance?

farce, and I chose to end my search for any kind of treatment. Instead of determining that I required treatment to help me in the "now", the therapists all seemed to focus on the "then".

I decided to return to handling the depression and anxiety that haunted me on my own.

During my absence of psychological care, I had mentioned my struggle to my mom. She thought that possibly I needed some spiritual help, and she made an appointment with her pastor's wife. Mom knew that this woman had a similar experience with sexual abuse, so she arranged a meeting with her.

My mom and I sat down on the blue upholstered seats of a pew in the middle of the sanctuary, and the pastor's wife seated herself in the pew in front of us. She turned around in the pew to face us so we could chat. I warily told her my story, edited, and void of details. All I told her was the fact that I had been molested for ten years, that I was struggling with it, and psychological help proved to be useless for me.

The pastor's wife then began to tell me that she had been molested as a child. She explained to me that the only way she gained peace about the matter was that she handed the struggle over to God. She then explained how she had prayed, naked on the bathroom floor, asking for healing of her heart and mind and spirit in all of her stripped down nakedness as she lifted herself up to God for His Divine Healing. Once she had made her plea to God, she allowed her faith to carry her through, and she was able to live a life that was not controlled by her abuser.

I listened to her story intently and it made perfect sense to me at the time. My mom and I thanked her for her time and her story, and we left in the hopes that her words and prayers would alleviate the anguish that I was experiencing.

I thought about the story of healing that the pastor's wife had told me. I relished the idea that it could be just that easy to rid myself of the demon that had already cheated me out of a normal childhood and was now just as unfairly raiding my adulthood. I spent some time soul searching and I determined that I would try the same approach as she did.

A few days later, prior to getting into the shower, I resolved to emulate the pastor's wife. I stripped my clothing off, kneeled on the blue shag rug on the bathroom floor and prayed. I prayed for the mass confusion that plagued my mind as I attempted to make sense of the violations I suffered to be eliminated. I prayed for the repulsively graphic images of the abuse that played in my mind like a vile horror movie to be erased. I prayed in desperation for the extreme sadness and disgust that I had for myself to be miraculously replaced with happiness and self-love.

I prayed for a miracle, with all of my heart, as I lifted myself to the Lord Almighty to heal me.

I was sprawled out on the cold bathroom floor with the complete nakedness of my body and soul, staring up at the blue flowered wallpaper on the ceiling through my tears of despair.

I anxiously awaited the answers to my prayers.

I suppose I expected an immediate miracle.

My heart felt like a heavy brick that I lugged around in my chest every day, becoming increasingly more cumbersome as my depression deepened. I didn't know how much longer I could feel that way.

I had sincerely hoped for instantaneous relief and received none.

I pulled myself together and raised myself off of the floor, and proceeded with my original plan of showering. I had lived with this hopelessness for as long as I could remember so the calculated actions that I took that day, although demonstrated in what I believed to be good faith, seemed not to have any redeeming quality.

My expectation of a miracle vanished as I continued to struggle through my days.

Chapter Seventeen

The Broken Glass Is Half Full

Once I graduated with my degree in Dental Laboratory Technology, I searched for positions as a dental lab tech. Because of my dental assisting background in addition to my lab tech skills, I found that the common answer from prospective employers after being interviewed was that I was overqualified for the position that was open.

I interviewed with an owner of a lab and he wanted me to come in for a working interview. While I was there trying to show off skills, the owner of the lab took every chance he could to touch me and it made me feel very uncomfortable.

I *knew* this touch, and it was an absolute violation.

Here was yet another older man who had chosen to put his filthy hands on me in ways that were unwanted and unsolicited. I never went back, and I made some flimsy excuse for why I could not work for him when he phoned me and offered me the job.

This experience was another on my growing list of infringements. It further solidified my feelings of vulnerability and inferiority.

I had worked so hard to earn a degree and start a career that I had undeniable skill and passion for. But, I chose to end my search for dental lab tech positions due to my experience during that working interview.

Fortunately, I was still employed part-time at the dental office near the city and my employer offered me my full-time position as a dental assistant back to me. I became more valuable to this dental office now as I offered an additional skill set.

About a year later, the dentist who owned the practice saw that it was necessary to close the office due to the neighborhood becoming increasingly unsafe. I started to worry about how my next job would turn out.

I did find a new position as a CDA in another dental office soon after losing my position. After working there only nine months and taking more verbal abuse, I was terminated from that position for made up reasons.

Woefully, I started yet another new job search, and just when I was feeling as if I made very poor choices in a career, I was called for an interview that changed my life.

***

In response to an ad for a dental assistant that I saw in the newspaper, I sent in my resume. I had been unemployed for approximately four months by this point and I had applied for all kinds of dental assisting positions, dental laboratory technician jobs, and been on countless interviews. It seemed as though my skill set didn't speak for itself like I thought it should. I received a call from a dental office to come in for an interview.

My first interview was with Lauren, the longtime office manager for the practice of Dr. Aleta, who was now looking for a new dental assistant because the assistant she employed for several years was leaving to earn her degree in dental hygiene. The interview went well with Lauren and I was called back to interview with Dr. Aleta.

It turned out that I seemed to be a perfect fit for the office and I was hired! I was excited!

I was very confident in my skills as a dental assistant and as a dental laboratory technician. I embraced any task I was given with passion. I would always try to complete a task with perfection, mostly because it caused me great anxiety to disappoint anyone, whether it was the patient or my employer. This anxiety followed me to my position with Dr. Aleta. The moment that finally began to alter that anxiety was during a mishap that occurred while I was still on a three month new hire probationary period.

In dental offices, as most who have visited a dentist knows, there is a suction that is used in patients' mouths. The fluids and debris that are collected by the suction travels through a main trap to filter out any

Chapter 17 ~ The Broken Glass Is Half Full

hard materials before it moves on into the sewer system. One of my duties was to clean out that trap.

The suction pump at Dr. Aleta's office was different than others that I had previously worked with. The removable housing around the mesh trap that collects all the junk was a glass jar that resembled a pickle jar. The ones I had experience with were made out of plastic.

I donned a pair of latex gloves and unscrewed the glass jar from the pump, removed the metallic mesh straining filter and cleaned out the scraps of filling material, chunks of tartar and other gross stuff. This was definitely not my favorite job to do around the office. Reassembly was as simple as reversing the disassembly, so, I knelt down in front of the large suction pump that sat behind two cabinet doors and attempted to place the mesh filter on and then the glass jar over it. In my attempt, the glass jar slipped out of my wet, gloved hands, hit the floor and shattered!

Mortified at the repercussions I imagined I would suffer for having to reschedule the rest of the day's patients due to me breaking the suction jar, I remained on my knees and began to weep. I summoned the courage to lift myself off of the ground and then meekly walked down the hall to face my dismal fate.

With tears tracking down my cheeks, and my nostrils filling up with snot, I stood in front of Lauren and Dr. Aleta. Woefully, I explained what had happened.

"We'll just have to order another one!" Dr. Aleta said with a chuckle.

She immediately called the dental supply company and ordered a new jar and directed Lauren and me to reschedule the rest of the day's patients.

In the nearly 15 years that I was blessed to be employed by Dr. Aleta, that story was told many times, usually after I made a sarcastic comment about something.

Laughing, Lauren or Dr. Aleta would ask, "Remember when she was so shy and she cried about breaking the suction jar?"

During the years that I was employed by Dr. Aleta, I tested her good nature. Although I never wanted to disappoint her because she was always so fair and good to me, there were countless days I was unable to go to work due to the depression and anxiety that I experienced. Somehow, she seemed to understand and still valued me as an employee and as a person. She had many conversations with me regarding my attendance, but I didn't change my behavior.

My absence affected the whole staff. Lauren would have to work double-duty, doing my job and hers. I would relentlessly fret about calling her in the morning to tell her that I was "sick". I knew the burden I was placing on the staff and the patients, but the "sickness" was stronger than the guilt.

My absenteeism due to anxiety and depression resulted in compounding my anxiety and depression.

Chapter Eighteen

Learning to Be Worthy

Prior to my job with Dr. Aleta, while I was in my early twenties, I met a man who was seven years older. He worked with Deanna at a gas station convenience store. I would go visit her while she was working a shift and sometimes he would be working, too.

As I got to know this man, I began to be attracted to him. He wasn't the kind of guy I would normally be attracted to, but he had a great sense of humor and we enjoyed hanging out together. We started going to movies together and we would hang out at his apartment and eventually we began going to church together. Before I knew it, we were dating.

I thought he was the total package, although I seemed to overlook a lot. He had a job, although not a good one. He had his own apartment, although he had no furniture. He had a truck that he said was his dad's, but had given it to him. He was "cute" and very charming…too charming. I believed he cared about me, so I tried to see his potential.

One night, we were approached by a police officer as we sat inside his truck that was parked on the lot of the convenience store he worked at. The officer wanted to know what our business was there and explained to him that he worked there and that we were just chatting. The officer asked for our drivers' licenses and walked back to his cruiser to check us out.

The officer returned to the driver's side of the vehicle where my new boyfriend was sitting. As the officer handed our drivers' licenses back, he looked square at me and said, "Young lady, did you know you are with a child molester?"

My heart dropped into my stomach. I couldn't believe what I was hearing! I looked at my boyfriend demandingly for answers as the cop left.

The moniker "child molester" sickened me. How on earth could

Who Will Save Me from Grandpa?

I be considering a life with a man who had done the inexcusable? Someone like my grandfather!

I awaited his explanation.

In his all-too-charming way, he told me that he had been wrongly accused of molesting a mentally challenged boy years before and had served a sentence in a mental hospital as punishment for the "alleged" crime. He convinced me that the abuse had never taken place and that the mentally challenged boy had lied about the incident. He said he accepted the sentence of time in the mental hospital in exchange for a prison sentence, and swore he did not commit the crime. I chose to believe him because I thought I loved him and that he loved me.

After that bombshell went off, we began talking about marriage. We sought counseling regarding our wishes to be wed from a pastor at the church we attended. At this meeting, I was surprised to learn that my boyfriend "used" to be gay and was delivered from his homosexuality by God. With my faith in God, I considered the possibility, made more excuses in my mind for him and began to make wedding plans.

My parents warned me of their suspicion about my boyfriend. They felt that there was something about him that was untrustworthy. I ignored their discernment and just assumed that they were trying to interfere with my happiness. I found out later that my whole family was so worried about this relationship they had considered an intervention to try to pull me away from him.

During the four months that we dated, he had countless jobs, mostly at gas stations and convenience stores and was fired from all of them because he was accused of stealing money. Of course, he denied all of these allegations.

Not only did he steal from his workplaces, he stole from me. He lied to me about new jobs he was starting and needed a new wardrobe. We shopped for clothing, I put it on my charge account and while I was at work, he returned the items and pocketed the money.

He sat on his couch in tears, and begged me for money to pay rent. I borrowed the money from a goodhearted dentist I worked with at the time and promised that my boyfriend would pay him back. He asked

Chapter 18 ~ Learning to Be Worthy

for money for food, items for his apartment, and many other things that I paid for while he went from job to job.

One morning, I woke up and the things I had learned about him over four months fit perfectly together like a puzzle. The culmination of the things I was told about him that he denied, the money that he used me and lied to me to obtain, the jobs he could not keep, the fact that he showed no romantic affection towards me including not even wanting to hold my hand, all pointed to the truth. He was everything I was told he was, but the truth was cloaked by my longing for love to believe it. He was a child molester. He was homosexual. He was a thief. He was a con artist who knew exactly how he was playing me.

I had to get out of this relationship.

I went to his apartment that morning with the intention of retrieving items that were mine and then ending the relationship with him, which is exactly what I did. I gathered my belongings that he didn't already return to the store for a refund, told him it was over, and walked out. On the way out of his apartment door, he screamed, "You're nothing but a fucking bitch!"

I just kept walking as more expletives were being hurled my way.

Once I reached my car, I buried my head in my hands and bawled. I was emotionally hurt but I felt liberated. I learned a valuable lesson in those four months. I would never again allow myself to be in any kind of relationship where I was a victim.

***

I spent a couple of years without being in a relationship, but I still pined for someone to love me. Of course, that same consuming depression haunted me as I attempted to find my path in life. I had changed jobs due to the closure of the dental office where I was working, and shortly after, I was set up with a man that worked with a neighbor of mine.

He was a very sweet, clever, and very intelligent man who was struggling to find his way, too. He had already served in the Air Force, and he wanted to go into aeronautical engineering, but there were financial and personal barriers preventing him from doing so. He rarely had a job and lived with his grandmother during the time we dated. But, I saw his potential.

We spent three years in a relationship off and on. We talked about marriage once but we both had different ideas of where our futures would lead us. I was the "house with a picket fence" type and he was a vagabond. Regardless of our differences, we loved each other.

Eventually, we realized our futures were not destined to be spent together, and we amicably ended the relationship.

I view the time that we spent together as a blessing because it helped me realize that I could be loved for exactly who I am, which I believe he did.

I found myself learning from my past relationships and I began to see glimmers of the strength and power of the strong woman that was buried within me.

I began to love myself for the first time.

Chapter Nineteen

Gifts

In late January of 1994, I was on a team in a bowling league on Wednesday evenings. I had joined the team a couple years prior with my co-worker, Lauren, when their team needed another teammate. Not too long after that we needed another teammate and my longtime friend, Lea, took the position.

I worked nearby, so once I was finished working for the day on Wednesdays, I would drive to the bowling alley, pick up a free monthly copy of a local newspaper to flip through while I waited for my teammates to arrive.

The paper printed local interest stories, ads for local businesses, plus a menu of which bands were playing at the local nightclub and concert venues. The paper also had a large personal ad section. I perused the personal ads occasionally to see if anything caught my eye. I answered one of them but nothing came of it, so I never answered another.

Nearing February, the publication was running a "buy one week, get a second week free" special for personal ads for Valentine's Day. Once Lea arrived to the alley I showed her the special. Many times we had joked around about placing an ad in to find a man. This time, we seriously chatted about placing ads and we both decided we would try it together. We both wrote our ads and sent them off to the publication and anxiously awaited the following week's paper to come out so we could see our ads.

I was careful to write my ad in a playful style, one that I would hope would attract someone to me that could see the "me" in it and be interested in contacting me

Who Will Save Me from Grandpa?

The ad read:

> **Free female puppy. Cute, blue eyes, long blonde, curly "fur", needs big, tall SWM for lifelong owner/companion. Likes to go for walks, play in the park and cuddle. Smart and very affectionate! Man's best friend. Letters preferred.**

I received close to thirty responses over the next several weeks, mostly written, as requested. There was a voicemail component to reply to the ad, as well, and I had only received one voicemail call which resulted in no message left, only a hang up. In those thirty or so responses, the range of the type of letters I received and their content varied greatly. I received a letter scolding me about how my ad was too revealing about me and that I must be weak and submissive to have written such an advertisement. I received a letter from a man who was a nudist and wanted me to go nude bowling with him among other nudist activities that he invited me to. I received letters from men describing their genitalia to letters that just listed a few likes and dislikes and their contact information, all seemingly intrigued by the "Free Female Puppy".

After reading each letter, I sorted them into a "yes" pile and a "no" pile, keeping all of them so I could read them again.

I contacted several of the men who answered my ad whose letters seemed benign and met a handful of them. I always met them in a neutral and public location, usually a restaurant to grab a meal or a drink together and chat a while. That is as far as the process would go. I either didn't feel a connection with them or they didn't with me.

While rereading through some of the letters from the "no" pile, I stumbled across a letter I initially rejected because the author was divorced and had a four year old child. I had convinced myself that I could not handle this kind of "baggage".

But this, by far, was the sweetest letter I had received. This man addressed me by name on the letter, which is something that was not revealed in the ad, but was on my outgoing voicemail. The letter

Chapter 19 ~ Gifts

also had a beautiful comment to a statement I made on my outgoing voicemail: The man I am looking for must know what true beauty is. I realized that this was the one person who had called and then hung up without leaving me a message! I reread the letter over several times and decided that I should call him.

This man's name was Curtis. I found him to be very sweet over the phone as we spoke briefly about ourselves and decided to meet each other. We chose to meet at a popular Mexican restaurant that was about a halfway point between each of our homes.

The restaurant was very busy. I arrived first and sat at the bar and ordered a strawberry margarita. I seated myself so I had a clear view of the entrance, and I nervously anticipated Curt's arrival.

We had not exchanged photos and only had given each other descriptions of ourselves prior to meeting. He had light brown hair that was parted on the side, wire framed glasses and a reddish-brown mustache. I knew him immediately when he walked through the large brown doors at the entrance of the restaurant. He walked towards me and because of the large crowd that was gathering at the bar, we decided to move our meeting to another venue that would be less populated and noisy so we could chat. We walked to our respective cars and I followed him down the street to another restaurant that wasn't as busy. We parked near each other and he exited his vehicle with a single red rose in his hand. As soon as I saw the rose, I teased him, "What? You had a rose in your car and you wanted to see if I was hideous before you gave it to me?"

"Umm," slightly embarrassed, he answered, "Yes!"

Curtis handed me the rose, we both laughed heartily and I hugged him in gratitude for the charming sentiment and then went inside the restaurant where we chatted until he had to leave to go to work that night.

I hugged him again once we were back at our vehicles and we chose to get together again on the Saturday of the upcoming weekend.

Our first "real" date consisted of us going to one of my favorite places, a conservation park where I loved going as a kid with my parents. We drove through, chatting the whole time, while looking

~ 73 ~

Who Will Save Me from Grandpa?

for the elk and the bison that roam through the park. We came upon a picnic table in the park and we decided to get out of his car for a bit. We both climbed up and sat on top of the table and chatted some more. We talked about everything under the sun…music, our jobs, his four year old son, our families…and I found myself scooting close to him as we sat there. Later, we decided on getting dinner and then we went back to the parking lot where I had left my car.

During our drive, a heavy metal song came on the radio, which I prompted Curtis to "turn it up!"

"I knew I liked you for some reason", he said. We had discovered we had the same taste in music, among many other things.

As our day together came to an end, we sat in his vehicle and chatted a while. By this time I had already figured out Curt was somewhat of a bullshitter. He had spent the day making me laugh with his sarcastic sense of humor so I didn't believe him when I asked when his birthday was and he responded, "April 26th".

"No way! That's my birthday!" I didn't remember telling him when my birthday way, but I figured I must had mentioned it to him on the phone when we first talked.

"Prove it!"

Curt handed me his driver's license and I scanned it for his birthday. It was April 26th!

As I handed his license back to him, I noticed his hands. They were well manicured yet strong and well lined, like mine. I showed him the many creases in my palms, and he held my hand as he studied it. He didn't let go…and sparks flew! I didn't know holding someone's hand would make me feel that way…all butterflies, giggly and excited. We talked some more as we held hands and made plans to see each other the following Tuesday.

We kissed goodnight and I started my trek home. I was "high" on Curtis. The actual drive home was a blur because my mind was swimming with the connection I had just made with this handsome, intelligent man. He was funny, kind, generous and gentle and I couldn't wait to see him again! I kept replaying our day together in my head and it couldn't have been more perfect.

Chapter 19 ~ Gifts

My dad was in the family room watching television when I came into the house. He asked how my date was and I told him that we had a great time. I told him that his birthday was the same day as mine. Dad chuckled and said, "That means something!"

He was right.

Curtis and I spent every moment we could together after our first date. Within two weeks, he felt comfortable enough to give me the key to his apartment and I didn't quite know how to handle that gesture, at first. I knew I deeply cared about Curt within days of meeting him, but I still kept my defenses up to protect myself from inevitable hurt. I was also trying to deal with the fact that he had been divorced and part of the "package deal" with him was his son, Michael. I wasn't sure I was ready to be in a relationship with a man with a four year old. I was very jealous of Michael. He received the attention that I thought I should have when we were together.

Very early in our relationship, Curt, Michael and I went to a park to spend the day climbing around on the enormous, round rocks that are found there. Michael was being a normal four-year-old boy and demanding attention from his dad and it was obvious to Curt that I was annoyed about it. Later that evening, after dropping Michael off at his mother's house, Curt had to remind me that if I want *him* in my life, I will have to accept his son, as well. All I could picture then was a life without Curt, which I did not want.

I had to realize that I had a very important role to play here. I had to play the role of a mother. The realization of this allowed me to know, without a doubt, that I wanted to be in both of their lives. I lowered my defenses, allowed myself to love Curtis completely and became a very significant influence in Michael's life.

The old adage that states that a person can complete another applies to my relationship with Curtis. The fact is, he makes me a better person for knowing his gentle soul. He has believed in me more than I could ever believe in myself through all of the years we have been together. He thinks I am amazing and beautiful, and he makes me feel as such. His desire to make sure that I am always provided for, loved, and happy astonishes me because I never expected that anyone could be so devoted Old because the one of the meds find me.

During the three years before we got married, we discovered many things about each other, one of which was the abuse I suffered and my lifelong battle with depression and anxiety.

One of the things that I believed made me not worthy of love was the abuse and how I felt it had damaged me. It was embarrassing to talk about, but I opened up to Curt about my past.

I found out that Curt was all too familiar with mental illness. He had spent his life watching his dad deteriorate from the sadistic effects of the disease. Curt explained to me that his was in and out of psychiatric hospitals and was prescribed different types of medications and therapies for years, to no avail.

Sadly, Curt's dad committed suicide after a couple of previous attempts. With this tragedy, Curt was given an understanding about mental illness that allowed him to understand my struggles better.

Although I never had the honor of meeting his dad, I am grateful for him. Along with Curt's mom, he helped raise this loving and compassionate man I am blessed to share my life with. I know he would be very proud of the man, husband and father that Curt has become.

Curtis and I were married on March 1st, 1997 in a beautiful church ceremony. We had one heck of a reception later that day, full of dancing and celebration with our family and friends. I felt like a princess who had married her prince and it will forever be the best day of my life.

Unquestionably, Curt is an absolute gift from God, and I believe he was sent to me to help carry me out of a very dark existence into a life where I am loved and supported beyond my comprehension. After all of the abuse I suffered and the resulting trials and pain I have gone through, I have been given something wonderful to assist in healing my heart.

***

Chapter 19 ~ Gifts

As I mentioned before, I was given the precious gift of my sister, Courtnie, in 1982.

I have always stated that Courtnie was the "me" that I wanted to be; a self-confident, unencumbered, uninhibited child who had a delightful personality that everyone loved. She insisted on being her wonderful self everywhere she went, usually leaving all who encountered her remarkable soul with a deep appreciation for her brilliant sense of humor and intelligence.

I was fortunate enough, most likely by divine design, that Curtis was placed into my life when I was somewhat older so that I could build my relationship with Courtnie. With the large age difference, it allowed me to help nurture her from newborn until I married when she was fifteen years old.

There came a time when I was tired of all of the stories being told to her by others that painted my grandfather in a positive light. Her impression of this monster was based entirely on these stories, and I waited until I believed she was mature enough to handle the information. Courtnie was thirteen as she sat on my bedroom floor, in nearly the same spot where Deanna revealed to me her secret. I was guarded in my delivery of the information by leaving gory details out. After I briefed her about the *real* grandpa, she told me that she felt like she had been deceived by all of the glowing accounts she had been told about him over the years.

Although I needed her to know the *real* "me", I didn't describe to her the dark places my mind had been over the years as a result of it all. Her existence had brightened that darkness.

Every moment I am honored to spend simply sharing sisterhood with Courtnie fulfills my life in many aspects. The unbreakable connection I am blessed to have with her soul is one I yearned for as a child but was gifted to me just when I needed it most.

Chapter Twenty

Shades of Darkness

Because of Curt's understanding of mental illness and his gentle nature, many times I have been in a deep depression or suffering from intense and agonizing anxiety, he has been my support system.

During an extremely pivotal point in living with the extreme depression and anxiety that seemed to build once Curt and I were married, the symptoms began severely affecting my sleep habits. I have always had trouble falling asleep, but now it was impossible. When finally dozed off, I woke up shortly after with my heart pounding in an absolute state of panic.

I began experiencing the inability to leave the house due to the immobilizing fear that something or someone was going to hurt me. I felt so vulnerable in my own home that I was convinced that as soon as Curt left for work, evil doers were lined up and trying to get in.

During this time period, a serial rapist was victimizing women in the city and surrounding areas. The rapist had been dubbed "The Southcity Rapist" due to the region of the city where the crimes were committed. Coupled with the media's incessant bombardment of these horrific stories of a man breaking into homes and raping women and the anxiety I was already dealing with, irrational thinking consumed my brain and I was certain that The Southcity Rapist worked with Curt and knew his shift schedule. As soon as Curt would leave for work, which included a lot of night shifts, I undoubtedly knew I was the rapist's next victim.

I would sit in our bed for hours, attentively listening to every noise, convinced that riding on every breeze was someone filled with evil planning to harm me. My eyes fearfully darted towards the perceived threat as my heart pounded violently in my chest. Anxiety enveloped me and I was unable to inhale deeply enough to fill my lungs with necessary air. I would quietly get out of bed in an attempt to peek

Chapter 20 ~ Shades of Darkness

undetected through the blinds on the windows with the hopes of seeing my alleged aggressor. I hoped for a glimpse of him before he could do the unthinkable. The intense raw emotions that engulfed me resulted in the escape of uncontrollable tears, thereby proving my vulnerability.

When I was finally able to slip into slumber, my dreams revealed the same scenario. I had no peace while I was awake, and I dreaded falling asleep because I would helplessly fall victim to the evil that would creep into my subconscious.

One morning, after Curt had come home from working a night shift, he crawled in our bed where I was still lying well past the time I should have been up.

"I guess you're not going to work again today", he said.

He knew what I was going through with my crippling anxiety and depression. He understood that I had not been sleeping, and that I was spending my nights having anxiety attacks. For some reason, his statement intensified the feelings of guilt I suffered from not being able to go to work and in that moment I began wailing and shaking violently. I fell out of bed onto the floor where I uncontrollably flailed my extremities. It wasn't a seizure or temper tantrum. It felt like a spontaneous combustion of the exhaustion, imprisonment and resulting guilt that I just couldn't bear any more.

I needed help.

I promised Curt that day that I would seek help. I couldn't hurt him like I know his father did when he took his own life.

The next day I contacted my medical insurance's referral service for psychiatric help. Interestingly enough, I found myself speaking with my sister, who worked with the referral place. She pulled some strings and managed to get me an appointment right away with a psychiatrist. This new doctor was very gentle and listened to me. He prescribed a couple different medications for depression and anxiety. He also wanted me to speak to a counselor and I proceeded to tell him of my past experiences with that type of therapy. He asked me to see this therapist one time, and if I thought it would be beneficial, then I could see her again.

I saw the counselor once, told her what I thought of counselors and then never saw her again. But, I took the meds, which seemed to help immensely. These medications didn't cause the same horrible side effects I had in the past, and after some time being on them, it seemed to keep my mood maintained at an even level. I was even sleeping better at night, mostly because one of the meds made me very drowsy and helped lessen anxiety.

This drug therapy made such a difference for me! Over time, I became more stable. I felt I could tackle college again to obtain my dental hygiene degree.

I informed Dr. Aleta about my desire to acquire my degree in dental hygiene. Her kneejerk reaction was, "Well, you know you have to show up to be a hygienist!"

I did not take her comment in a negative manner, although I was hoping for her support. I understood what she meant, but I believe that her comment was partially because she would lose me as her assistant if I did.

Shortly thereafter, I enrolled in college.

I took my prerequisite coursework at a community college, and then was accepted into a dental hygiene program at a different college to finish my degree. As I always did in college, I set out to thoroughly succeed. I already had an extensive pertinent education and skill set, and this seemed to be the natural progression of my career.

Curtis was by my side in my endeavor. He was the perfect supporter and my biggest fan. I was able to utilize his astounding intelligence when it came to my algebra and chemistry classes, since I struggled with those at first. I spent many times with my books and papers spread all over the dining table with by head in my hands and tears of frustration streaming down my face while Curt gently explained to me how to solve for x or balance a chemistry equation.

Fortunately, due to my own maturity and a brilliant and patient husband who was able to love me through my sobbing and low self-confidence, problem solving in these courses finally clicked, and I was able to go forward with the classes and ultimately made very high "A"s.

I did tend to come home and complain about tests I had taken when I "only" scored a ninety-eight percent. I would get very upset with

Chapter 20 ~ Shades of Darkness

myself because I always expected perfection. Of course, Curt would chuckle and say, "Oh, you are one of *those* people!"

Once I began college courses full time it was necessary to end my full time position with Dr. Aleta in 2000. I worked as her assistant on weekends and time off from classes. Once I earned my degree and attained my license she wasn't able to employ me permanently, so I moved on to another office. Once in a while I filled in for another hygienist in her practice. It was always fun to go back and work with her and see patients that I had known and treated as my family for many years.

***

I excelled in college. I earned a high GPA, was honored with leadership awards, academic and clinical honors awards, President's List, Dental Hygiene National Honor Society, and other awards. After all of my intensive studies and clinical practice, I scored the highest mark possible on the clinical board examination, and I scored the highest score in the history of the college on the National Board Dental Hygiene Examination.

I had never achieved so much in my life, and my success was due to my ultimate desire to succeed…for myself.

Once I graduated and had my license in hand, I obtained a position as a Registered Dental Hygienist in an office where the dentist was more interested in retiring than in treating patients, but it was a good place to start and hone my skills.

During my second year practicing there, I began having severe pain in my left ankle. I noticed a large, egg shaped swelling on the inside of this ankle. It was very uncomfortable to touch and it had become horribly painful to walk.

Years before I began having this new pain, I had fallen down a set of stairs and severely sprained this ankle. Surgical intervention was deemed necessary at that time and resulted in ankle reconstruction. I consulted an orthopedic surgeon for diagnosis and treatment of this new ailment. After an MRI was performed, my doctor found that as a

~ 81 ~

result of the repetitive trauma to that ankle, a ganglion cyst had formed and was wrapped around some nerves. The treatment plan was surgical removal of the cyst, which I promptly scheduled so I could find relief of the excruciating pain I was experiencing.

After the surgery, I acquired a nasty post-operative infection. The oral antibiotics my doctor prescribed seemed to have no effect on the infection, so he needed to operate again. He re-opened the surgical site, cleaned the wound and stitched it closed. Treating this infection required me to stay a few extra days in the hospital with strong antibiotics administered intravenously. Once I was released, my surgeon prescribed different oral antibiotics for me to take. Unfortunately, I continued to suffer a series of infections and I had to endure five more surgeries over a three month period, which meant more hospital stays, and rounds of IV and oral antibiotics. After the fourth surgery, I had to administer intravenous antibiotics at home for a month through a PIC line.

I believed I was finally on the mend. After three months of being in and out of the hospital, going under general anesthesia multiple times, dealing with post-operative pain and the resulting infections, and being on a museum of antibiotics, I was beyond ready to get on with my life, be healed and get back to work. My incision was nearly completely closed and was healing well. Unluckily, I was caught in a sudden torrential rainstorm at a Labor Day celebration at a park. Within hours of being knee deep in rainwater after the severe storm, my surgical site became extremely swollen and severely inflamed and painful.

The following day I went to my surgeon on an emergency basis and he immediately scheduled surgery. He opened my ankle for the fifth time and left it open to drain, which bought me more days in the hospital.

I was appointed an infectious disease specialist who informed me of the results of the bacteria that were cultured from the latest infection; I had E. coli and other fecal bacteria growing in my ankle from the contaminated rainwater.

I had never had an adverse reaction to needles or medical treatment

Chapter 20 ~ Shades of Darkness

prior to this deluge of infections and surgeries. I had always felt fairly calm when it came to having any kind of procedure. But after bearing the physical pain of being incessantly impaled with needles, experiencing complications with general anesthesia, enduring post operative pain, suffering extreme nausea from narcotic pain meds and the compounding stress multiple surgeries tends to put on the human body, the trauma of all I had gone through had taken its toll.

The thought of undergoing one more procedure was more than I could take.

Three days after my surgeon re-opened my acutely infected ankle, I was in pre-op again waiting for a nurse to place the customary IV catheter, preparing me for yet one more surgery to clean the wound and then subsequently close the offending site. My surgeon decided to leave the wound open this time and he packed it with gauze to allow for drainage for three days, with plans to follow up with this final surgery. Five nurses, one anesthesiologist and my surgeon all made multiple unsuccessful attempts to start an IV. Following the repetitive torture, I helplessly laid on the uncomfortable hospital bed, openly weeping with my body riddled with blown veins. My whole body was trembling from the painful attempts and I begged them to stop. My surgeon and the anesthesiologist agreed their only option was put me under anesthesia through the PIC line I had in my arm, and then start an IV once I was asleep. Thankfully, this idea worked, and my doctor was finally able to close my ankle.

After this wretched experience, I gained a severe intolerance to any kind of medical procedure. I could no longer watch surgeries on television, whether real or fake. The beginning sequence of the television show *E.R.* was enough to push me into fits of panic. All that I had experienced with this one ankle had traumatized me in a way that I never thought possible.

During this time of numerous surgeries, hospital stays, and infections, I was unable to perform my job for four months. This undoubtedly caused me a great deal of stress. I was so worried about losing my position and not being able to financially contribute to our household. Curt was ultimately forced to be the sole supporter of our household. Fortunately, the job he had at the time offered him plentiful overtime hours.

The time off I had taken due to these surgeries put my position at risk due to the necessity to employ a new hygienist to take care of patients in my absence. When my ankle had healed enough to go back to the practice, my position had been given to the person who had filled in for me. Although I was offered a part-time position to return to the practice, I chose to leave and seek a full-time position. I had weighed my options and I realized that the dentist I was employed with did not share the same philosophy or integrity that I had regarding patient treatment. It was time to move on.

I took hygiene positions in several different practices, and they all had one thing in common…none compared to working with Dr. Aleta. Several of the practices were only interested in production rather than focusing on patient care. In some cases, the integrity that I possessed was on trial by the very people that hired me for that quality. I wasn't going to tolerate being taken advantage for the sake of having a paycheck. I knew my worth when it came to my skills as a dental hygienist and I refused to sacrifice patient care for greed that controlled the practice.

I have always stood up for what I believed. I may not have always had the courage to vocalize my view about my convictions, but as I found out, the more often I mustered up the nerve to speak my mind, the easier it became to defend myself. I was learning that it was up to me to protect myself.

I worked hard to get to this point in my life. I had overcome many obstacles emotionally for these achievements.

The improvement in my patients' oral health and overall health was what I strived for. With my manner of educating patients, my knowledge and my skill set, I did just that with my patients. I gained so much satisfaction in taking care of these people like they were family, some of them became like family.

I loved hearing, "You are the best hygienist ever!"

Nobody knew that every single day I functioned within the consuming fear of making a mistake. I was always on guard, expecting

Chapter 20 ~ Shades of Darkness

to be confronted by a co-worker about something I may have done wrong. The only benefit of feeling this way is that I learned at a very young age to be a perfectionist as a way to ease my suffering.

***

  I had been practicing dental hygiene at a federally funded health center for several years in a position I dearly loved. Working in public health seemed to be my niche. I felt honored to be able to take care of the underserved population, offering them services they could not afford anywhere else. Unfortunately, that ganglion cyst in my ankle reared its ugly head again and I needed surgery to remove it…for the eighth time. I had to take a couple months off to heal and nearing the time when I would have been able to return to my beloved practice, I received a letter terminating my employment, stating falsehoods that led up to it. I was furious! I had done so much for this facility and for lies to be told about me that resulted in me losing my job was just despicable. I was extremely upset, but within weeks, I received a call from Lauren at Dr. Aleta's office. She told me that Dr. Aleta had fallen ill and had other dentists filling in to treat her patients until she would hopefully be able to return. Then she asked if I was working anywhere and when I told her that I wasn't, she offered me a position there. I immediately accepted the position, knowing that I would get to go "home" and treat patients that I had known for years and hope that soon Dr. Aleta would be able to return to her practice. Ultimately, she had to sell her practice because her illness proved to end her ability to work. Sadly, Dr. Aleta and I never had the opportunity to practice together again.

  I never had another job that compared to working with this compassionate, caring soul that I was blessed to love as a friend. Dr. Aleta taught me an immeasurable amount about how to treat people in the kind manner in which she approached all of her patients. I affectionately considered her as my mother-aunt-sister-friend who accepted me with all of my faults. She made me more proficient in my profession, and she made me a better person, all by simply being in her presence.

This brilliant, witty, kindhearted and beautiful woman who touched every soul she encountered sadly left this world in 2009 after her battle with a long illness. There is not a day that goes by that I do not think of her fondly, and I eagerly anticipate the day we will be reunited so I can tell her personally how she touched my life.

***

In 2006, Curt and I moved to a brand new home. I was working steadily at the time, and he had recently accepted a position as a Union Representative that required him to travel every week to service the Locals he was assigned. The house that we were living in for the first nine years of marriage was located in an increasingly unsafe neighborhood near the city. I no longer felt secure in my home, and I had been verbally accosted on several occasions while in my own yard. Out of necessity, our search for a place in this world where I would feel comfortable, or as comfortable as someone with an anxiety disorder could feel, led us to purchase a beautiful new home about 60 miles south of the city.

Having a clean slate of a home was a big change from the total rehabilitation of the house we had moved from. I had always dreamed of starting fresh in a newly constructed home, and I was thrilled to use my creative talents to decorate it. I named my style of décor "vintage eclectic" due to my conglomeration of tastes that didn't fit neatly into one category. The biggest compliment I ever received in appreciation of my home interior decorating skills was from my sister-in-law, Natalie. She had been with us through the purchase of the home, as we hired her to be our real estate agent, and had seen the house's bare bones. After a couple months had passed, she and my brother came to a family gathering at our house and she commented upon walking in that it looked like a display home! I was honored by her compliment and I have had many other compliments regarding my ability to coordinate

Chapter 20 ~ Shades of Darkness

décor, along with a vote of confidence from several friends who asked me to help them decorate their homes.

Curtis and I both enjoy working outdoors in the yard. I love the physical aspect of gardening and the creative aspect, as well. I carefully planned and executed landscaping around our home and it created a welcoming and comfortable place for Curt and me to live in a small lake community with a picturesque view of the water.

It appeared that I was living the dream. I had a career that offered excellent pay and benefits, a beautiful home on a lake, a husband who loved me beyond my understanding who worked hard to help provide for us, our two doggies and four felines. I was blessed with family who loved me, and caring and supportive friends, yet my reality was a constant struggle with ever-increasing depression and anxiety.

Not only was I dealing with depression and anxiety, I had been bombarded with diagnoses over the years. Diabetes, high blood pressure and a multitude of surgeries all took their toll. I underwent a hernia repair, a tonsillectomy and adenoidectomy, eight ankle surgeries, a gall bladder removal and a hysterectomy. I also dealt with severe chronic back pain since I could remember and suffered migraine headaches. I took a handful of pills daily and had to inject insulin several times a day to treat and maintain the hand I had been dealt. Most days I felt awful, both physically and mentally.

I had starting looking for a new job. I never had difficulty finding a position as a RDH in the past, but for some reason, I was struggling. I had sent out nearly one hundred resumes within the metropolitan area, some had positions open and some I sent cold. I had no clue what I could possibly be doing wrong in my job search or during the few interviews I had. Curt was becoming increasingly concerned that we were not going to be able to pay our house payment without my salary contribution. I was working just a day and a half for the dentist that bought Dr. Aleta's practice and that pittance somewhat helped, but it was no match to the salary I previously brought home.

I had no interest in doing anything except sleeping. I did not want to get out of bed. I had no ambition. I had no energy. I did not want to be with my friends. I did not want to go to work. I did not want to exist.

Who Will Save Me from Grandpa?

The medication I was taking for depression and anxiety seemed to have stopped working, and I was afraid to try another new antidepressant after the liver damage debacle I dealt with previously.

I distanced myself from everyone and everything as I spiraled farther and farther into the dark hell that is known as depression. I seriously began contemplating suicide once again.

Contemplation of suicide was something that was normal throughout my existence. Even as a child, I wanted to die. Being devoured by overwhelming anxiety and debilitating depression was customary in my daily life. The pain was so excruciating that I could see no way to manage it except to eradicate myself.

It had always been completely normal to feel as if all of the breath in my lungs had been forcefully sucked out of me through my toes while I struggled to take my next breath. I believed that it was perfectly natural that my heart felt so heavy that I could barely stand erect. The copious tears that would sting my cheeks were shards of my broken psyche. These unbearable feelings were multiplied by my views of worthlessness and self loathing. I felt locked in an internal prison with no escape. I believed wholeheartedly that people were inherently evil and that many were plotting to hurt me. I was certain that others were in constant judgment of me. I was engulfed with a relentless fight or flight sensation during my waking hours and during the few hours I was able to sleep, vivid dreams filled my mind with malevolent imagery.

I felt I had a justifiable reason to die.

Chapter Twenty-One

Darkness...

While in our twenties, Deanna's and my relationship had become strained. She had distanced herself from most of the family during her life's struggle as a result of the sexual abuse that she suffered. Her path, in her attempt to deal with the pain and embarrassment that resulted from the abuse, took her into many treacherous places with terribly dangerous people.

Her disconnect from me was heartbreaking. We seemed to be pulled in different directions. I had married a wonderful man and she was in an extremely abusive relationship. The more time passed, the more estranged we became.

Several years went by that she and I didn't speak. I knew of her relationship with a crack addict who abused her mentally and stole from her financially and emotionally. She kept her distance from much of our family because she was aware of how we all felt about her seemingly chosen situation.

Deanna somehow found the strength to pull away from this horrible man and she slowly came back into my life, which I am ever-so-grateful for.

Curt and I had lived in our home for a couple years when I had invited Deanna and her sister out to swim in the lake. This would be their first time at our new home and I was anxious to see them, show our home to them and enjoy our time together.

I asked Deanna to come out another day soon, which she did. This time, it was just the two of us, and we finally had time to chat with each other. Something we had not done in years.

I told her of the severe depression that I was currently suffering, and that I was in the throes of thoughts of suicide again. We had conversations of this type in the years prior, but in those conversations, we spoke of our mutual feelings of disdain regarding the abuse.

Who Will Save Me from Grandpa?

This discussion was different. Deanna went on to inform me about some treatment she had recently completed with a trauma recovery program at a university near the city. She explained to me that it was a research program where trained therapists administered testing for Post Traumatic Stress Disorder, and if the patient met the criteria to participate, they would receive a particular therapy for PTSD. She mentioned that the program would pay the participant a nominal sum of money to help reimburse fuel costs to travel to the school two times a week for twelve weeks. She told me of how they had helped her, and she encouraged me to call them.

The money the program offered was an incentive. I was only working a day and a half practicing hygiene while I continued to search for a full-time position with no luck. With working such limited hours, I certainly had plenty of time to spend going to the multiple appointments to be part of a research program. But, regardless of this, I neglected to call for an initial evaluation.

As weeks went by, I remained in a severely depressed state. I had received a phone call from Deanna, who was following up with me to ensure that I was seeking placement in the trauma recovery program. I told her about my procrastination and she encouraged me to contact the facility once again.

Just as Deanna coerced me to promise her that I would inform my parents of our grandfather's violations after she revealed to me that she had also suffered his abuse, she compelled me to take an oath that I would call the trauma recovery center.

I fulfilled my promise soon thereafter and made an appointment for my initial visit.

On September 22nd, 2009, I arrived at the trauma recovery center. I filled out the obligatory paperwork and met with a trained therapist who conducted my initial interview. I was told that the purpose of this particular project was to study the effectiveness of two different types of therapy for the physical and psychological effects of crimes on victims.

The interview lasted for five hours, and then I was asked to write a very detailed description of one memory of abuse that deeply impacted

Chapter 21 ~ Darkness...

me. All of the information they gathered during the interview along with the memory I was to write about is how they were to determine if I fit the criteria to be a participant in the program.

I had no idea what memory to write about. There were ten long years of too many events to choose from, and it was difficult to pick just one.

Suddenly, a memory came blazing through to the forefront of my mind. It was the memory of my grandfather molesting me on his pontoon boat, going home and finding out that I had started menstruating and then having him comment about how I "felt wider down there". This was most likely the most impactful incident of the lot of them.

There so many memories that had haunted me my entire life, intrusively replaying inside my head like a pornographic horror flick. I worried that since we were only focusing on the one memory, the other appalling memories would not get the full attention they deserved. I expressed my concern to the therapist, and she consoled me that one was all that was needed for this study and that, hopefully, the therapy I would receive would help me deal with other memories.

A few days later, I received a call, stating that I was accepted into their trauma recovery program and I set up my second appointment with them to complete their assessment.

This round of assessment included tests designed to measure physical responses to the memories of my abuse, such as my heart rate, my startle point, and other signs of stress. One test included listening to a recording of someone reading the memory that I had written the previous visit. Another test required me to view images while my response to each one was recorded, and another where I submitted myself to listening to silence through headphones for an undetermined amount of time and then disturbed repeatedly with surprise loud blasts of a siren sound. Once they collected their data, I was reappointed to begin therapy.

The therapy I was assigned was Cognitive Processing Therapy (CPT). This therapy was designed to help me understand ways that the abuse has affected my functioning, such as my feelings and beliefs about my own safety, my trust in others, and my ability to have close relationships. I was to discover how my beliefs since the abuse led to my symptoms of depression, anxiety, fear and general distress. I would then learn how to alter these beliefs.

Once I began therapy, I was told that the results of the assessments I had completed determined that I was suffering from Post Traumatic Stress Disorder. I was completely shocked at this revelation since my understanding of PTSD was much like the general public's, in that it was a malady that affected war veterans or people that had experienced violent crimes.

I was informed that the therapy I was to receive was not going to be easy as it involved many repetitions of reviewing the memory that I wrote about, basically reliving the abuse that took place during that one event multiple times. I learned that the way this exposure therapy works is that it allows my brain and my body to feel the emotions that I *should* have felt and processed years ago. Much like a person needing to go through the stages of grief in order to heal, there is a process in healing from trauma.

The idea of having to relive that event over and over produced severe anxiety and absolutely horrified me. I did not understand how this type of therapy would be beneficial, but I was at my rock bottom. I was living in a depressed state so much deeper than I had ever experienced. I had to follow through with this therapy, or I would probably die by my own hand. I could not put Curt through that after what he dealt with from his own father committing suicide.

I was willing to try the therapy since Deanna had success with it, and I believed I owed it to her to carry out what she deemed as very helpful to her.

Reliving the event I chose to focus on was agonizing. In fact, in the beginning stages, the therapy deepened the depression. It put the abuse in the forefront of my life and increased the all-too-frequent flashbacks that I already endured. I was informed that this could happen, but I chose to be strong and believe that relief was pending.

The work while at the trauma recovery center was intense, and I was assigned plenty of homework designed to help with my recovery.

Chapter 21 ~ Darkness...

Several of these assignments involved writing the memory over...again. While writing this memory, I was to include any sensory details that I could remember that took place during the event, and I was also to document the physical reactions I experienced as I completed the assignments. Prior to going to each therapy session, I was to reread the account again. It was important that I allowed myself to feel the emotions and physical sensations that accompanied reading and writing the event repeatedly.

The assessments and therapy sessions were usually audio taped or videotaped so the researcher could score the tape for accuracy, and use for research and training purposes. At first it was odd to be captured in this manner, but after a while it became a normal part of the therapy appointment.

Chapter Twenty-Two

...Into Light

One facet of my therapy included working through the automatic negative thoughts and unpleasant emotions that I would experience regarding situations and the world around me. I would complete worksheets that step by step forced me to challenge these strong negative beliefs or conflicting beliefs.

I was taught that because the abuse took place during such a critical period of my mental development, I had not learned how to view the world or my place in it in a healthy fashion. The overabundance of negative events in my life resulted in negative thoughts and emotions that I attempted to neatly fit into my life as being *normal*. I had a lot of work ahead of me to finally process the warped thoughts that constantly bounced around in my brain.

I realized through this therapy that the absolute fear and vulnerability I felt just being out in the world was *not* normal thinking.

My view that everyone is inherently evil and plotting against me caused mistrust and constant vigilance, resulting in intense anxiety to do even the most simple tasks, like walking from my car into a store.

I believed that all older men were sexually abusing their granddaughters, and every time I crossed paths with an older man I was filled with disgust and intense flashbacks.

My fear of making a mistake and the repercussions that would follow caused extreme anxiety.

I convinced myself that when my husband gave me a certain "look" he was getting ready to tell me in his next breath that he was leaving me, causing me intense anxiety.

Chapter 22 ~ ...Into Light

I was positive that when I felt an intense surge of anxiety that I was going to die, which just exacerbated the anxiety.

I felt that my life was ruined by my grandfather and that there was no hope for me, so why live?

I believed that all things were in my control and if something bad happened it was my fault. I took on guilt for these things.

There was no doubt in my mind that sex was ruining the world since it seemed to have ruined mine. News reports and other stories seemed to confirm my belief.

These examples are a glimpse of the "all or nothing" and exaggerated views I had about the world. These were my automatic thoughts because I because I let the emotions I felt when these situations happened determine my thinking. If these thoughts made me feel a certain way then they must have been true in my mind. I completely disregarded other important aspects of the situations that triggered these thoughts. It made for an overwhelmingly fearful and anxiety laden world for me to live in.

This process of challenging my thoughts seemed painstaking and time consuming at first, but practicing the technique has made it become second nature. I can testify to its merits in learning how to cope with day to day unpleasant emotions and thoughts in any situation.

This technique of challenging beliefs, and the exposure therapy that I (sometimes) reluctantly took part in, proved to be my SALVATION.

I began to notice a strength in myself which EMPOWERED me.

I started to feel UNENCUMBERED by the constant fight or flight feeling, which had always been my natural state of existence. Once that feeling decreased, I found it difficult to understand the strange, peaceful emptiness that my body felt. The feelings of high alert started to ease and my mood was now elevated. I felt PEACE for the first time.

The heavy iron shackles of a very painful and long imprisonment had finally been removed, and I was feeling the beautiful, warm sunlight on my face again.

My psychiatrist reduced my dosage of the antidepressant because I was doing so well. Unfortunately, this was done while still in therapy at the trauma recovery center so my contribution to the research became null and void due to the necessity to stay stable on medications for accurate research. Nonetheless, the center allowed me to finish the program, and the therapy that I received was absolutely life changing.

I was asked to write about my feelings post treatment by my therapist:

> "The sexual abuse I endured certainly affected my life, but as I see things now, I have more control over those affects.
>
> This negative succession of events in my life, the way it was handled once it was revealed to my parents, and the impact it made on my thinking and development, were all completely out of my control. I was an unprotected child and I could not have changed any of it, even if I tried. Absolutely **NONE** of it was my fault.
>
> I feel fortunate that I was given this chance **(FINALLY)** to resolve the issues that have left a mark on me and helped change the negative thinking patterns that developed from trying to deal with the trauma.
>
> I did not know until recently that my way, the **OLD** way, of thinking was so wrong. All of these years I believed everyone thought the way I did. I had no idea the impact that the abuse had on my thinking. I feel now that my mind has been uncluttered and free of the constant negative thoughts.
>
> Yes, the trauma happened. I cannot change that. But now, my feelings about the events have

Chapter 22 ~ ...Into Light

faded. My anger has faded towards the abuser and the people that did not handle the situation the way I thought they should. I am no longer dwelling on 'how I was wronged'.

I feel better about myself, my environment and being safe in it. I no longer feel as though people are constantly judging me or trying to hurt me. I have a better understanding of what things I actually do have control over and I do not seem to get upset when I am unable to control things, such as the idea that I need to be 'perfect'. I know that the world will not end if I do not have control over a situation.

I am a worthwhile person with a lot to offer. I am smart, attractive, funny, caring, creative, loving, and generous plus so much more. I do not have to constantly prove that I am these things to myself or others.

In general, I think all people have good qualities and there are some out there in the world who make it a point to hurt people. I think that I will still run into people like that throughout my life, but I know now it is not everyone's agenda to be hurtful. I have learned that some people may be hurtful and do it out of ignorance, selfishness, or other reasons I may not understand, but the entire population of the earth I no longer believe is 'inherently evil'.

I am now able to catch the thoughts that used to cause me to plummet into depression and anxiety and work with the thoughts before they can negatively affect me. I am able to minimize anxious feelings to a more manageable level.

> **There are a lot of things in this world that I do not have control over but know I can identify what I can realistically control and let the rest happen."**

I certainly learned many things during the process of my recovery from trauma. I had no idea that I could feel so free. I left the program with a new sense of self and a positive outlook. As I left my last visit with my therapist at trauma recovery center, I was reminded that the skills that I learned must be practiced post treatment to hone and maintain them, which made perfect sense at the time.

I remember walking out the door of the center for the last time. A refreshing, cool breeze gently caressed my face as I exited the building. Seasonal fallen leaves swirled around my feet as I walked to my car. I sported a new self-confidence that I had never worn before and I was happy to be part of this new day!

Chapter Twenty-Three
Negativity Breeds Negativity

I reveled in my fresh outlook on life. I felt happier and more at ease than ever. The persistent intrusive thoughts and flashbacks of the abuse that had always crowded my mind had considerably decreased, freeing it from the prison that was created by the control that was imposed upon me. My abnormally high startle point still existed but was lessened, resulting in a calming of the constant feeling of being on high alert. The hell I had lived my entire life at no fault of my own no longer had complete power over me. My family and friends noticed the difference in my demeanor and self-confidence, although most did not know of my recent treatment at the trauma recovery center. I did not tell many people that I had gone through treatment for PTSD because I knew that they would not understand my affliction with the disorder when I could hardly believe it myself. I figured most people would think that Post Traumatic Stress Disorder affects those who have seen war or brutal violence, just as I did prior to learning the truth about it. I chose not to explain the fact that I had suffered traumatic events repeatedly for ten years and I finally found treatment that worked for the depression and anxiety that consumed me for so long.

***

The health issues that I battled for years and I took multiple medications for required me to visit my physician routinely. Shortly after completion of my initial treatment for PTSD, at one visit with my physician, I mentioned to him that I was having a lot of issues with extremely painful abdominal cramping and severe diarrhea. He prescribed an increase in my fiber intake, which didn't help and my symptoms worsened. Severe abdominal cramping along with a constant urge to evacuate my bowels kept me on the toilet much of the day, doubled over and rocking back and forth, just to have blood and mucous come out. I generally felt physically ill most days.

I was referred to a gastroenterologist who performed a colonoscopy. His diagnosis was that I had ulcerative colitis. My own body was now attacking my colon as if it was a foreign object.

I was prescribed several medications to treat this auto-immune disorder, one being a medicine to suppress my immune system so that my body might stop attacking my colon.

Many days when I was scheduled to work, it was necessary for me to call my employer and tell him that I was too sick to come in. I would have to scramble to find another hygienist to cover my shifts so my patients wouldn't be without care. This happened so often that it impaired my relationships with my patients, co-workers and employer.

When I was at work, I would be treating my patient, but the excruciating cramping and intense urgency would make me break out into a sweat and I would have to excuse myself and run to the restroom.

After calling off of work for the umpteenth time, I received a phone call from my employer. He was a very nice man and he was as gentle as he could be when he told me that from a business standpoint, he had to terminate my employment due to my inability to regularly attend my scheduled hours. I wholeheartedly agreed with him, and my termination became more of a mutual agreement. I needed to focus on taking care of my health.

It was very hard to sever my relationship with this dental office because I was leaving behind a friend and co-worker, Lauren, who I had known since the day that I started working for Dr. Aleta many years before. I also felt like I was abandoning the many patients that I was honored to treat, whether they were longtime patients that I had treated for years that had been transferred from the sale of Dr. Aleta's practice or patients I began seeing at this office.

My lack of success in my lengthy job search began to make sense. I wouldn't have been able to keep a job with my health issue. Even though I was too ill to work, I kept sending out resumes to prospective employers. I could not accept the truth that I couldn't practice my beloved profession.

Chapter 23 ~ Negativity Breeds Negativity

I had spent over twenty-five years learning and honing my skills and I had always been dedicated to being the best that I could be... for me, my employer and my patients. I defined myself through my profession. Having all that I worked for and loved suddenly stripped from me left me feeling like a worthless failure.

The idea that I could not contribute to our family financially was an additional stressor that I certainly did not need. I was not equipped mentally to deal with all of these new changes in my life, and I began sinking into depression again.

While I was slowly responding to treatment for ulcerative colitis, I was dealing with chronic back pain. I had dealt with that pain since I could remember, but it was worsening. I sought out diagnosis and treatment for it and several radiographs and an MRI later, I was diagnosed with degenerative disc disease, spinal stenosis, and disc impingement, which validated the chronic back pain that I had experienced for many years. Added to the mountain of medications I already was downing daily, a new anti-inflammatory and physical therapy was prescribed. The prescription NSAID barely took the edge off the pain and the physical therapy was generally a waste of time.

Feeling physically ill and dealing with chronic pain every day is not any way to live. It was difficult for me to make any kind of plans with anyone because I never knew how I was going to feel. I had to cancel many plans with my husband, family and friends.

In addition to feeling as if I had an alien-ninja-scissorhand-baby dancing around in my intestines, I began to feel severe body aches that resembled the muscle aches that present with the flu. I didn't have any other flu-like symptoms, but these horrible muscle aches would leave me lying on the couch, moaning in pain...every day. My skin was so tender that I could not tolerate my clothes to touch it. My hands hurt so badly that washing my hair or my body in the shower became difficult. I had fatigue that I had never experienced before and the pain was emotionally and mentally maddening. I truly began thinking that I could not live with the intense, incapacitating, sickening pain that I was in much longer. I absolutely had to find some relief, if there was any.

Thoughts of suicide began surfacing again. I had lost my "purpose" when I lost my ability to work, and being ill and in pain constantly left me feeling absolutely worthless.

***

I sought answers for the relentless body aches I was experiencing. Several specialists later, I was finally diagnosed with fibromyalgia. I found out that many times, people who have auto-immune disorders are also diagnosed with fibromyalgia.

I was thrilled to have a name for what I was dealing with! This news presented me with a small amount of hope that I finally might get some relief. I was prescribed a medication, which somewhat helped, but only at higher doses. The medication kept the fibromyalgia pain at a dull roar, at best. I still suffered days of debilitating pain from fibromyalgia and the many other structural ailments, but my life became a bit more tolerable by way of my ever-growing arsenal of pills.

Just when I thought I could breathe and slowly ease into a homeostatic level of remission of ulcerative colitis and somewhat manageable fibromyalgia pain, I began feeling a strange pressure against my trachea, like an outside force was pressing on it. I saw my family practitioner for my normal follow up and I told her what I had been feeling. She ordered an ultrasound on my neck. With this ultrasound, it was determined that I had some calcifications in my thyroid gland, so off to a new specialist I went. She ordered a biopsy.

With my history with multiple surgeries, tests, injections, images and so on, medical procedures are not new to me. But, I was not prepared for what a needle biopsy of my thyroid gland entailed. Without any kind of anesthesia, a needle was repeatedly inserted into my neck, guided only by ultrasonic images and was maneuvered through the fibrous glandular tissue.

"You're doing fine," the nurses and the doctor assured me. If fine meant horrible, then yes, I was fine.

Just when I thought they were done, the cytologist said there weren't enough cells in the sample to make a diagnosis with, so on with more impalement.

Chapter 23 ~ Negativity Breeds Negativity

Finally, the doctor gathered good samples with all of the painful skewering and they dressed the site and gave me an icepack for pain and swelling.

I vowed I would never subject myself to any procedure like that again without some kind of anesthesia or tranquilizer.

Then we waited.

***

I was standing in the jewelry making supplies aisle at a craft store with my creative juices flowing while I sorted through strands of beautifully glistening beads when my mobile phone rang. It was the specialist who had ordered the biopsy. She began explaining to me the results of the biopsy and revealed what I never expected…*I had thyroid cancer.*

The cancer was not only in places in my thyroid, but one lesion was growing outside of my thyroid. Her recommendation was to schedule surgery as soon as possible for a total thyroidectomy.

I was alone when I received this life-altering news. I was still trying to recover from the mental and emotional impact from the cascade of crap that had already took control of my body. This news made my head spin. I stood there, solitary, with my phone in my hand. I felt hollow.

I called Curtis. He had left earlier that morning and was still on the road traveling for work. Teary-eyed, I spoke the same words that the doctor said to me.

I explained it all very clinically to him, trying to be stoic. With my background in dentistry, I had a pretty good grip on medical terminology. I didn't want him to worry about me since he was going to be gone for the week and I didn't want to traumatize him with this news. He had already lost his mom and his grandma to cancer, so naturally, his mind went *there*. He was devastated. He was worried about me being alone, but I worried about him being alone, too. We talked about the treatments I would need and he did his own research online once he reached his destination, which helped him understand my situation much better. He is out of town most weeks with his job

Who Will Save Me from Grandpa?

and this compounded his stress, not knowing if he would be able to be with me for my upcoming procedures. I couldn't wait for him to get back home in a few days so I could hug him.

I called Mom and Courtnie to tell them of the news. They didn't want me to be alone, either. So, we met and spent a few hours together talking, laughing and crying.

I had a certain peace about the upcoming surgical procedure itself, but it turns out that my perception was wide off the mark regarding the effect of having my thyroid removed. I thoroughly underestimated how I would feel for weeks following surgery. It was necessary to have my thyroid hormone levels deplete to allow for successful uptake of the radioactive iodine to kill any remaining thyroid cells. Post-surgical discomfort was gradually replaced with hypothyroidism, which resulted in extreme fatigue and brain fog. Every movement I made was a chore. I was so lethargic I could barely function. Just to pull myself off of the couch to feed myself was difficult. I couldn't hold a thought but for a few seconds. I was in "hypo-hell".

When my thyroid hormone levels were finally low enough, I was obliged to swallow a capsule of radioactive iodine and be sequestered to my bedroom for seven days so I wouldn't contaminate others. Courtnie was able to stay with me to make my meals and take care of my pets and the house since Curt had to be out of town.

Spending time with Courtnie is always a hoot, whether I am in the same room with her or stuck in my bedroom for a week. I would wake up in the morning and ask for a cup of coffee. Since I was behind closed doors to prevent any contact with anyone, a wooden TV tray was set up as a valet for food, drink and such right outside my door. I would open my door after she communicated with me that she had my coffee on the tray and I would open the door and find a foam cup with the brew, light and sweet, just the way I like it.

On these cups, she would use a Sharpie and write something clever on them. The first one she had written "RADIOACTIVE SISTER" with the universal radioactive symbol drawn on it. Another morning I opened my door to a cup that she had written "FOAM CUPS GIVE YOU CANCER…oh wait…" on it.

Chapter 23 ~ Negativity Breeds Negativity

I looked so forward to my morning coffee, more for the cups than the coffee! I would take pictures of the cups and share them on social media and my friends would look forward to them, too!

***

After the surgery, preparing for the radioiodine treatment and the treatment itself, the question "Why me?" crossed my mind constantly. Why I was chosen to endure the level of agony that had been unfairly distributed to me? I realized the constant bombardment of new diagnoses and the other stressors that were now part of my life were triggering those oh-so-familiar feelings of high alert, depression, anxiety, thoughts of suicide and absolute worthlessness.

As I struggled with my body to get better, I continued getting worse.

I began having severe pain in my hip joints upon walking. I had been tolerating it for months, knowing I could only walk very short distances until the agonizing pain would stop me in my tracks and cause tears in response to the excruciating pain to stream down my cheeks. Once I would stand still for a few minutes, I could walk another short distance again. I had attempted to self-diagnose the reason for the agonizing pain, most likely due to an aversion to seeing yet another doctor.

After a while, I realized how much the debilitation was interfering with my daily life so I decided to see an orthopedic surgeon to assess my hips. After more radiographs and injections and MRIs, it was determined that I had torn cartilage in both hips, which could only be repaired by surgery. The doctor refused to do any surgery on me because I already had too many other medical issues. He wanted me to be a year outside of the thyroid cancer diagnosis and be clear of it before he would consider doing it.

I was left to continue to endure the severe, piercing pain and the debilitation that accompanied it.

Not long after coming to terms that I was destined to have the hip pain for a while more, I began having disturbing heart palpitations and dizzy spells. Standing up would cause me to be on the verge of "blacking out". I had a normal pulse while standing, but when I sat down, it would drop too low.

My heart was flopping around my chest so much that I couldn't sleep.

After weeks of these strange sensations and spells of near fainting, my symptoms became worse. I phoned the emergency room of a nearby hospital and told them of my symptoms. Their recommendation was to come in and be seen as soon as possible. I called a neighbor friend of mine and asked if she could take me to the hospital since Curt was out of town for his work.

I was admitted to the hospital on the cardiac floor with my newly found arrhythmia. My heart wasn't pumping enough blood to my brain.

My cardiologist ordered a stress test, which showed no disease, so the next step was an electrocardiologist. Another hospital stay and an unsuccessful electrophysiology study later, the treatment was another medication to help control the arrhythmia. The medication did not work and it was necessary for me to have a pacemaker implanted.

***

After being struck down repetitively with medical issues and surgical needs, with many of the multiple medical conditions inundating my body within a three year time period, I never was given time to adjust to the rapid change in my health, physically or mentally. I found myself sinking increasingly deeper into depression and being consumed by unbearable anxiety, despair and overwhelming surges of impending doom. Disturbing flashbacks of the abuse I suffered were forever filling my mind yet again, inaccurate thoughts were becoming more and more frequent and automatic, and the peace I worked so hard to achieve had waned. The walls of that familiar prison were closing in on me and I realized it was time to seek help again.

I had been seeing a psychiatrist for medication management for several years. She had witnessed the positive change in my mental health as a result of the treatment I obtained at the trauma recovery

Chapter 23 ~ Negativity Breeds Negativity

center. I expressed the way I had been feeling to her and she was concerned about my lack of stability and downward turn. She promptly referred me to a facility where there were multiple practitioners. I was appointed with a doctor who evaluated me and then referred me to another psychologist, Dr. Brook.

I explained to Dr. Brook my history as a victim of sexual abuse, the lack of any kind of treatment for many years, and the ineffective efforts by other mental health care practitioners. I told her of my positive experience at the trauma control center and the onslaught of changes in my health that I had relentlessly encountered over such a short period of time. I listed all of the health changes that had now caused my inability to work and how these factors have progressively revealed my feelings of worthlessness and deficiency. I presented the details of the deepening depression, the escalating anxiety and the frequent enveloping sensations of impending doom and despair that I was suffering.

From experience, I was aware that finding mental homeostasis can be extremely taxing and would only yield results if I was dedicated to the cause. I knew I had to be willing to confront the baneful demons that seemed to have power over my existence. I was willing to perform the work necessary to find my way back to the peace that had slipped through my fingers at no fault of my own. Realistically, there had always been much more "work" that I needed to complete after my first experience with trauma therapy, but since I had such a positive outcome then, I believed I could continue to ride that wave.

I never considered that life would throw so many changes at me and rouse all of the pain that controlled my life for so long.

It was time to take my power back.

Chapter Twenty-Four

Revelations

My days consisted of inaccurate thoughts that would cause me to be upset, anxious, depressed, scared, angry, and judgmental. I had no proof that the thoughts I was having were true, but my mind would run with the thought and take me to very negative places.

Curt and I had gone to dinner at a casino buffet. We enjoy playing video poker once in a while, and we had a "two for one" coupon to eat, so it was the makings of a rare evening out.

While we were sitting in the dining area, I noticed a particular elderly man who was seated at a nearby table with whom I believe was his wife. He was a large man who had a full head of longish, white hair, a deeply creased and pock-marked face. He was wearing a red plaid flannel shirt which was open in the front and allowed his crew necked white undershirt to be visible, and a pair of overly large, faded-out jeans that were well cinched with a belt underneath his protruding round belly. He did not resemble my grandfather in the slightest way, yet upon my initial peek at the man, a fiery feeling of disgust swelled in the pit of my stomach.

My distorted perception convinced me that he was molesting little girls.

I pondered his wife's possible knowledge of the things her horrible husband was doing to little girls, viewing her with a mixture of sorrow and disgust. I felt pity for her attachment to this horrible man and then hatred for her for allowing his crimes.

The loathing I felt towards this man consumed my thoughts, erasing any enjoyable time I was experiencing while out to dinner and well into hours afterward.

These types of thoughts and feelings compounded exponentially with every older man that crossed my path, invading my thoughts with

Chapter 24 ~ Revelations

sickening flashbacks and causing my focus to stray and my mood to plummet; controlling me, sometimes for days at a time.

I experienced overwhelming thoughts about others I would encounter on a daily basis, believing that each had a secret agenda and was covering up despicable acts, only to reap some personal benefit. These beliefs I had made me feel incredibly vulnerable. I was certain that I was going to suffer some kind of physical or psychological attack.

I was on high alert at all times. The crippling anxiety I felt was like the initial gasp of air one takes when suddenly frightened but with no subsequent exhalation of that breath.

In addition to the onslaught of negative thinking about others and situations that I was experiencing, beliefs of my complete worthlessness engulfed my thoughts as well. I would become furious with myself for "allowing" myself to think these horrible things about other people, which was proof to me that I was the one that was a terrible person.

In a true vicious circle, the multiple health conditions that I had accumulated in such a short period of time were the catalyst of the mental distress I now found myself with and realized I needed to seek help for. The years I internalized the stress from the harm that was done by my grandfather surely resulted in the battery of my body, leaving it broken and in pain. A person cannot possibly affect someone in such a negative manner and not leave their victim with an array of ill-effects.

One of the first matters that Dr. Brook guided me with was to learn acceptance of the fact that there was a myriad of health conditions that I co-exist with. The chronic pain and other health issues that I believed diminished my worth and caused my inability to work became rampant and controlling factors of my daily life.

I handed over my power to these illnesses as they thieved every remnant of self-worth that I had worked so hard for.

Together, Dr. Brook and I defined the qualities that I possessed in my positions working as a dental assistant and practicing as a dental hygienist over the years. Outlining the ways I functioned in these capacities helped me understand that on a broader scale, I have always lived my life as a caretaker; in my professional life and in my personal life. I had spent many years in a very specialized manner offering the finest care of the many patients I had the privilege of treating. I had always made protecting and taking care of my family and friends a priority. Not only did this recognition of my character help me understand more about myself, *I understood my purpose.*

I learned there are multitudes of ways I can practice being a caretaker, and doing so does not have to be part of a career, result in a paycheck, or even demand physical work. Simply put, having loving thoughts, intentions and actions are functions of a caretaker. I need to consciously practice this daily but is very rewarding by renewing my self-worth and allowing me to serve my true purpose.

What is more important than love? What a wonderful purpose I have in this world! This enlightenment helped me be more at peace with my body's limitations.

Dr. Brook helped me learn that I am not my body and that I can simply just observe the way my body is feeling without giving power to the pain or illness. She tells me that our bodies are "just vehicles that our souls use for transportation". She always has a brilliant nugget to share with me and helps point me the right direction.

The practice of "just observing and not giving power to" is extremely liberating.

Serving my purpose has centered my being and has permitted me to focus on regaining the power in all aspects of my life and, in turn, unlocks my mind for more healing.

Chapter Twenty-Five

Exposure

It seems there are many reasons why people who are afflicted with depression, anxiety, PTSD or other mental illnesses do not seek treatment. Finding a doctor or therapist that can treat these specific conditions effectively, financial constraints, believing mental illness is a weakness, fear of being judged, and the knowledge that therapy can be very intense, uncomfortable and a lot of hard work can be barriers.

I can personally attest to knowing that relief from suffering with these mental illnesses is available and can come in many forms, such as prescription medication, therapy (of many types), a strong support network, and spirituality.

Many times we hear stories about those who have become drug and alcohol abusers, prostitutes and attempted or committed suicide only to realize later that at some time in their pasts they have been victim to some kind of sexual abuse.

In retrospect, I am confident that I would have eventually succeeded at committing suicide had I not continued to seek treatment repetitive times in my adulthood. The pain of living in my own head and barely functioning as a daughter, sister, friend or wife could have been easily snuffed out by a well-placed bullet or a perfectly executed collision with a rock wall.

Numbing my mental anguish with drugs or alcohol could have certainly been an option if I did not have the need to maintain, or at the very least appear to maintain, control.

***

Some of the PTSD symptoms that I suffered from were disturbing memories, nightmares and flashbacks of the abuse. I found it difficult to experience joy and happiness. I was tortured with relentless anxiety, which kept me at an elevated state of alert. Incapacitating feelings of impending doom would wash over me. I was irritable, angry and I was very easily startled. I had difficulty falling and staying asleep and I had no interest in things I used to enjoy. I avoided places that reminded me of the abuse. When I would experience these symptoms, the physical responses would conquer me. In order to reduce my pain, the easiest thing to do was to avoid thoughts and feelings about the abuse.

As I found out, when engulfed in the prison of PTSD, I was living in the past. It was very hard for me to be present in the moment, which in turn, led me deeper into the sinister pit that I existed in. Dr. Brook taught me the importance of being mindful and living in the present. I learned that whenever an upsetting thought, memory or flashback began to wrap its evil, tormenting fingers around my mind, I needed to bring all of my senses back into the present moment. A technique I was taught to accomplish this is to be mindful of the position of my body. For example, examining how the chair feels as I sit in it as my body presses against it, being aware of the temperature of the room and determining its comfort level, interpreting the sounds around me and focusing on how the air feels inside my lungs as I deeply inhale. I found making sure I practice this technique daily continues to build the skill and makes it readily available as I need to use it. The practice also reinforces that I have power over the intrusive thoughts that have crippled my mind for so long. When my mind would fall into the downward spiral of anxiety or flashbacks, I could now lessen or even stop the thought before it would send me reeling into the dark chasm of full blown panic.

During several appointments with Dr. Brook, while speaking of the abuse and experiencing the deluge of flashbacks due to the nature of the discussion, I would refer to the "little girl" that would stand in the corner of her office. This child was approximately ten years old, appeared very broken and defeated, as her head would hang atop her slouched, rolled shoulders. She emitted such a palpable deep sadness and I felt such incredible compassion and love for her. She would hopelessly peer upon me with her wide, pleading eyes. The overwhelming urge to help this poor little girl be free of the obvious pain she was experiencing enveloped me.

Chapter 25 ~ Exposure

This little girl was me.

I realized that when I saw this little girl, I was allowing the malevolent flashbacks and upsetting memories of the abuse control my mind and to have power over me. I fought these frequent flashbacks and thoughts with a gentle reminder from Dr. Brook that I was here in the present, in her office and I was safe. I was no longer that dispirited little girl and I chose to take the power back that was unjustly stripped from us as a child. She did not have that option; therefore it was my responsibility to help heal her.

Upon the acceptance of the facts surrounding the abuse and truly believing it was at no fault of my own, but also understanding that I was now safe and I had the power over the damage that was done, I slowly became whole again. Eventually, the young "ghost" of myself slowly faded back into me, setting her free. I love her and she deserved to be a little girl, unbound from the control of the abuse she suffered.

Since I had success with exposure therapy at the trauma recovery center, Dr. Brook suggested that I pick up where I left off with that type of therapy. She had me begin writing one of my memories of the sexual abuse. Like before, I wrote the event in great detail. Then I had to succumb to the repetitive reading of what I had written, allowing my mind and my body to process the event by feeling and experiencing the emotions and thoughts that I should have when the events happened. Once exposure to the event did not evoke a strong response of anxiety, disturbing imagery, upsetting thoughts or flashbacks, I could move on to another of the many vile acts in which I was forced to play victim.

I prepared myself for the increase of frequency and intensity of upsetting mental imagery, intense flashbacks, massive mood swings, fiery anger, deepened depression and increased anxiety. The upside is that I knew that this increased amount of negativity was temporary until the exposure therapy did what it was intended to and helped heal me from that event of the abuse. I found that the downside to completing and healing from the event was the awareness that I had so many more events that I needed to work through to continue to heal. I had tremendous anxiety about the transition from working on one event to another, but I was committed to the purpose and I continued to stay the course because I knew the outcome was absolutely worth it.

I had finished working through an event with exposure therapy and it was time to choose another to work on. Dr. Brook and I discussed what would benefit me next and I introduced to her the sickening physical response I would experience when driving by a roadside park. This was a place that my grandfather would take me as a little side trip after shopping. He had found it to be a usually desolate place, which was perfect for him to molest me in his car.

In addition to the roadside park, other visual triggers resulting in upsetting imagery, flashbacks and thoughts would present themselves daily. Many times I would drive the same roads that my grandfather would travel with me while I was his naïvely willing captive. A simple drive by the lake community that my grandparents resided, and visits to certain parks and towns would activate distressing memories and feelings that would consume my mind and body.

I was instructed by Dr. Brook to *not* avoid these roads or places but instead, be mindful of how I was feeling at the time and let that feeling flow in and flow back out like a wave. I was not to give these thoughts control by being present and to have an awareness that nothing bad was happening to me at that moment.

My next exposure therapy assignment was to go the roadside park that sickened me every time I rode past it, pull into the park, park my car and sit. I was to try this for short periods of time and increase the time as I could tolerate it. I decided that since I visited Dr. Brook weekly that I would make the trip to the roadside park on my drive home from my appointment with her.

I set out after my appointment to begin my newly assigned exposure therapy. I entered my car and drove approximately forty-five minutes to the roadside park. I reluctantly pulled my car into the crescent-shaped drive-through road of the small, empty park that was dotted with a few decaying picnic tables and trashcans. Once parked, my eyes nervously darted in all directions as my anxiety increased. I fidgeted, trying to find a comfortable spot for my rear end on my leather car seat. My mouth went dry as my heart rapidly pounded in my tight chest.

Chapter 25 ~ Exposure

Although it was a nice, warm spring day, I kept my windows tightly closed and my doors locked along with keeping my engine running in case of an urgently needed escape. I tried to bring my thoughts to the green leaved trees that graced the other side of the picnic table area. I could only spend mere seconds focusing on the leaves swaying from the tickle of the warm breeze and then I would torturously be pulled back into the painful anxiety and anticipation of another horrific crime against me.

The anxiety became so overwhelming that I put my car into gear and quickly sped away to seek relief from the agony that I had just subjected myself to.

The following week at my therapy appointment with Dr. Brook, I described to her what seemed to me as a failed attempt at facing one of the demons that continued to have such a tight grasp of my psyche. She reminded me that it can be a painful process and encouraged me to continue my trips to the roadside park for exposure.

I did as she instructed, trying each time to become more comfortable with the environment, reminding myself to use the coping tools I had learned. I slowly became more comfortable in opening my passenger's side window, but the driver's side window had to remain closed. It was just too adjacent to where I was seated and might allow free reign for whatever evil that lurked on the other side of the tempered glass to seep in.

I would watch the squirrels twitch their fluffy, gray tails in play and confidently jump from tree to tree. I noticed that although the trashcans were full of garbage and encircled with inquisitive yellow jackets, I never saw any other visitors while I was there.

I continued my therapy at the park for several weeks and noticed only a small reduction in the intensity of the anxiety that I experienced while I was there. I was never able to exit my car and could not fathom the idea of rolling down my driver's side window during my visits. I continued to feel extreme dread when I knew I had to deliberately drive to that unkempt, wretched place. In this case, exposure therapy left me feeling terribly vulnerable and exposed to certain danger.

As I sat in my car for what resulted in my very last visit to the

Who Will Save Me from Grandpa?

abysmal place, I practiced my normal routine: I parked my car along the side of the asphalted crescent-shaped drive, slightly rolled down my passenger's side window that faced the park area while leaving the driver's side window securely sealed. I scanned the trees for the clown-like squirrels to entertain me.

While I was intensely attempting to stay focused and present, lending my senses to listening and watching the wind rustle through the leaves of the many trees that lined the length of the park, I glanced into my rearview mirror and was startled to see a white SUV pulling up behind me. I noted that the driver was an elderly man, which immediately prompted fear and dread to engulf me. With my heart fearfully pounding, I quickly rolled up my window and turned the ignition key, positioned my right foot on the accelerator in preparation for a quick exit from my car's resting space as soon as I could get it in gear.

As I apprehensively gazed into my rearview mirror while I geared up to exit with haste, the man walked around the back of his vehicle and then to the rear passenger side door. As my anxiety escalated exponentially, he opened the rear passenger door and out jumped a cute little beagle! In that moment, still with an adrenaline rush of terror coursing through my body, I realized that the man was not here to harm me but to let his little doggy play. I watched as the man took a seat at one of the rickety picnic tables so he could comfortably watch his furry companion happily prance around.

I finally exhaled the last shallow breath I had been holding since I first saw the man pull up in his vehicle behind me.

I watched the pup for a moment as it happily played but the anxiety that had just taken complete control of my body was now resulting in an outward symptom; I began bawling. I had to leave the roadside park that very moment.

I was done.

I was done with forcing myself to go sit at this park where my memories are of my grandfather molesting me in his car.

I was done with the crippling anxiety I felt while I drove there and as I sat there.

Chapter 25 ~ Exposure

I was done with being encased with complete vulnerability as the seconds ticked by until "I had done my time" at the park. The tiny amount of anxiety reduction regarding that miserable park, regardless of how many times I attempted to reassure myself of my safety, did not seem worth the torment I was forcing upon myself.

I was done with the anger about the abuse.

I was done with it *all* and I had had enough of the constant barrage of negativity that filled my days and nights with only the hope of healing my broken mind.

I conceded to the power of what my grandfather had done to me and I felt like that was my only option.

The following week, I informed Dr. Brook that I absolutely could not continue the exposure therapy regarding the park. I explained to her the reasons why and then described how I was incredibly physically, emotionally and mentally exhausted from carrying around the burden that I had been unjustly given to bear for the rest of my life and from trying to banish all of the demons that were left behind from the abuse.

I described for Dr. Brook what the burden was to me as I vividly painted the very large, brown burlap sack that I strenuously lugged around with me everywhere, every moment of the day. This sack was completely crammed full of rancid, foul smelling *shit*. This hefty collection of fecal material represented all of the negativity, pain, vulnerability, abuse, hopelessness, despair and anxiety that I was doomed to drag around with me forever. This bag seemed to be what defined my existence and how I felt about the world and about myself. This sack, sickening as it was, had my weary fingers gripped tenaciously around its neck for as long as I could remember, without release.

I told her I could not continue to carry this cumbersome, revolting burlap container of all that has maliciously attacked my thought process, self-esteem, relationships, self-worth, my days, my nights, my health and my career.

She asked me, "Can you set the bag down and walk away from it?"

Believe it or not, the thought of losing the vile, smelly sack in that moment literally terrified me. It had been such a fundamental part of my existence my entire life, I could not imagine ever being completely without it.

"No," I answered. "It is part of *me*."

"Can you empty the bag?"

After giving her last question some thought, I decided that I could try to lighten the load of the sack.

Then, in my mind, I emptied as much of the foulest waste that I was comfortable with at that moment by realizing just how far I had come on my journey of healing. The sack became a small degree lighter.

Once I thought more about her question, I realized this collection of detrimental negativity that completely engorged this bag had shaped my life and dictated so many of my thoughts and reactions. It had power over me for too long.

My *dead* grandfather, who created and filled that sack, *was still controlling me*. Giving my power away began to make absolutely no sense to me. It was time to take *my* power back by releasing the accumulated contents in that foul sack.

Over time, I expelled the contents of that exasperating bag, and what was left was a not-as-stinky, crusty, shit-lined sack that had become significantly lighter. I still had the same grip around the neck of the bag but because of its reduced weight, the bag became less cumbersome as I carried it. I accepted the fact the contents had shaped my life and now carrying it seemed no longer a burden.

I realized the purpose of the sack; it helps me serve *my* purpose, which is the writing of this book

***

During the same appointment with Dr. Brook when I started emptying the iniquitous sack, came another very impactful component of my journey of healing. I had stated to her, during my woefulness of my failed attempt of my latest exposure therapy, I wished I could view myself the way others tell me they do.

She asked how I felt other people close to me view me.

Chapter 25 ~ Exposure

"Well, they tell me I am smart, funny, creative, and helpful...and that I am awesome."

With the assignment of lessening the load of the sack and a mutual decision for me to take a much needed break from exposure therapy, she gave me my next therapy assignment...TO BE AWESOME.

That was all. I was to be the awesome *me* that I was designed to be. I was to be awesome to myself and take care of myself so I could be awesome to others and fulfill my ultimate purpose here on earth, which is to be a blessing to others. From this simply beautiful concept came a renewed purpose, enthusiasm and empowerment. The simple idea that being the awesome Child of God that I am *is enough* was liberating and truly amazing.

Chapter Twenty-Six
Peace, Love and Awesomeness

Once I had started "practicing" being awesome, since it was not a concept I was accustomed to, I began to identify the unique characteristics that make me the awesome Child of God that I am. I found a very healing part of being awesome includes viewing others as the innocent and truly awesome Children of God that they are.

Being able to love someone enough to only see their soul is very trying at times, but this view has removed shackles from the way that I present myself, the way I interact with others and how I view others. I am aware that viewing others in this manner will forever be something I will have to consciously work at but it has certainly become more natural for me. I believe we are designed to view each other in this way. Learning how to see others in this loving, non judgmental way has filled me more peace than I believed was possible here on this earth.

***

My mom and her brothers would speak about my grandfather… their dad…in my presence, *a lot*. They would talk about him in such a reverent way, as if he did not repetitively rape two of their own children.

Every time they would do this, it made me feel worthless and extremely angry that I still did not matter.

One of the reasons I chose not to speak of the abuse with my parents, even into adulthood, is that I felt it was **my** burden.

I have always tried to protect others from physical or emotional pain. I feel deep empathy for all living beings and it tortures me to cause any suffering.

This was an issue that I struggled with for as long as I could remember, and it was a subject that I presented to Dr. Brook during a therapy session to work through.

Once we spoke about it, she helped me realize that other people

Chapter 26 ~ Peace, Love and Awesomeness

are in charge of their own feelings. By protecting my parents, I was shouldering all of the pain.

She introduced me to the concept that my pain is just as important as other people's pain. Dr. Brook then mentioned that if I would be able to discuss this issue with my mom, that it could ease some of my pain.

Of course, my first thought was, "THERE AIN'T NO WAY!" I figured I would suffer some wrath by doing so. After I thought about it for a while, I told her I would try.

Within that same week, during a normal conversation with my mother, somehow divinely the conversation presented me with a perfect opening to practice what I had recently learned about others being in charge of their own feelings and that my pain is important, too.

I explained to my mom how uncomfortable it made me when my grandfather was spoken about in front of me.

My mom responded, "I didn't know it still bothered you like that."

I don't think that my mother understood how much it "bothered me like that" because I have always diligently worked at appearing stoic and unencumbered.

But, I wondered how they could not know that the mere mention of him would make my blood boil in anger. The fact that my mother and my uncles would speak of him as if he was some sort of hero made me physically ill. Their references of him usually happened during family gatherings where others would be having a good time and I would have to fight with upsetting imagery, thoughts about how he so negatively affected my life and confusion about why they insisted on speaking about the horrible man who committed crimes against his granddaughters and who knows who else.

Several years ago, my whole family went to dinner to celebrate Curt's and my birthday. As we were sitting at a long table at the restaurant, I overheard my mom say to my brother, Corey, "When my dad worked as a truck driver, he would…"

I elbowed Courtnie, who was sitting to my right, and with a chuckle I said, "Hey! You know what he used to do to me?"

I believed everyone else should view him as I did.

Here I was in my mid-forties and I felt disregarded and unprotected.

~ 121 ~

It was difficult for me to understand that the other lives that surrounded my grandfather, outside of the ones he sexually abused, had been touched in a manner that did not shatter their world.

Others' memories were of a grandpa, a father, a husband and a brother. He was a friend, a neighbor, a truck driver, a hunter and a fisherman.

I learned that I should not condemn them for seeing him as these things. Our different opinions and feelings toward him were built on our own experiences with him.

For so many years I had focused on the sins he committed against me and saw him as a monster who thieved my childhood, tainted experiences in my life, and pushed me into very destructive behaviors.

I found it extremely difficult to humanize him.

Dr. Brook suggested that he was created as a perfect soul…an Innocent Child of God.

I struggled with that notion for some time. I felt like if I viewed him in that way, ultimately I was giving him permission to do all of the horrible things that he did to me.

We talked extensively about forgiveness and how forgiving my grandfather would be a pinnacle of my healing. I truly believed I would never get to that point.

I had always considered forgiveness as pardoning someone who has wronged me, resulting in my internalizing the offense to in the attempt make things right…to benefit the offender. Dr. Brook introduced me to the concept of what forgiveness truly is, and at first, it was extremely difficult to grasp.

Forgiveness is simply acceptance that a wrong has happened. It does not absolve a sin against a person but allows the person who was wronged to maintain their own power over the event and provides peace for them.

Forgiveness is seeing the person who has wronged another as the Innocent Child of God that they are, stripping them down to their pure soul and loving them as that pure soul.

Forgiveness is unadulterated love.

Over time, the concept made sense. I began considering these

Chapter 26 ~ Peace, Love and Awesomeness

things and realized there was much more to my grandfather than what I chose to focus on.

Once practiced, forgiveness has created astonishing peace within me and has significantly reduced my suffering.

***

I realized how far I have come in my journey of healing when I recently went to place flowers on some relatives' graves during the 2015 Christmas Holidays with Mom and Courtnie. It is something we like to do together when we can, kind of a "girls' day out". We have lunch together, laugh, remember those whose final resting places we are visiting...but I usually dread when we visit my grandfather's grave.

He is buried at National Cemetery because he was an Army veteran. My grandmother is buried in the same grave and her name is on the back of his marker.

I love going to this cemetery because of the history that is in place there. It is a beautiful place, well-kept with seemingly infinite rows of grave markers perfectly in line with each other. There are also large herds of deer that roam the place and Mom had brought along some apples that had seen better days that we could feed to them. (She knows how much I love animals!)

It has bothered me for some time that he was honored by being buried there. That cemetery is for heroes, not child molesters.

As we visited other family members' markers, Mom shared her memories of them while placing glitter-sprinkled silk poinsettias affectionately at the base of the stone.

Mom remembers where her loved ones are buried by landmarks within the vast cemetery. She drove around and found where her parents are buried.

I tried to stay present and just enjoy my time with my mom and sister.

We got out of the car and walked up to the back of the grave where my grandma's name was engraved. While I was standing there, the cold

Who Will Save Me from Grandpa?

December wind was whipping my hair around and made my eyes water while I stared at her name.

I watched my mom place a seasonal bouquet on their grave and then lovingly pat the stone that identified them. I could see the pain of loss in her eyes, which saddened me.

Courtnie watched our mom's movements and they saddened her, as well.

When I thought neither one of them were looking, I meandered to the other side of the tombstone and casually glanced at the name engraved there.

I expected to cringe. I expected to feel nauseated. I expected to be angry.

I felt nothing.

It was the first time I had no physical reaction when viewing his name in this cemetery. In fact, I really felt more of a reaction because I felt so neutral about it!

Later on, I mentioned to Courtnie how I glanced at his stone and didn't feel any negative feelings about it for the first time ever.

"I know. I saw you."

I was glad she witnessed my peace.

***

During the same conversation when I finally told my mom how it would make me feel when my grandfather would be spoken about in front of me, I felt it was time to reveal to her that I was writing a book about my experiences with child sexual abuse.

"Mom, I want you know that I am writing a book about what grandpa did to me. I didn't mention it before because I didn't want to destroy the family." (I was still in the learning stages that others can be in charge of their own feelings.)

Wincing, I awaited her knee-jerk, defensive response of disappointment.

"He has already done that!" she exclaimed.

Chapter 26 ~ Peace, Love and Awesomeness

She followed this unexpected response with her blessing regarding the book.

After time, I realized that this one conversation lifted a great strain on my relationship with my mom. I found that suppressing this burden for so long in order to spare her from pain and then revealing it was particularly healing.

My relationship with my dad I would not deem strained, but distant. I never feared or mistrusted my dad but the distance I placed between us was undoubtedly an effect of the abuse and a safety mechanism.

I have always envied other daddy-daughter relationships, including my sister's relationship with our dad. I have always said that I "worship the water he walks on", but I have always wished for a closer relationship with him. I have spent most of my life feeling massive guilt I never took the initiative to foster a closer relationship with him.

Another gem that Dr. Brook suggested, "Don't you think that if you were capable of nurturing a closer relationship with him, you would?"

I am so grateful that God put this brilliant and genuinely caring woman in my path!

It took me a long time to realize that I have done the best I could with my relationship with Dad. The constraints that were unfairly put in place will never change the fact that I dearly hold him in my heart and love him beyond words.

***

My attempt to crawl out of the multifaceted prison that was created by being a victim of childhood sexual abuse would have been impossible for me without proper and effective help and therapy. Undoubtedly, my ultimate demise would have been of my own hands.

My lack of a support system, fear of disappointing my parents, worry of judgment, tremendous shame and my refusal to speak about the abuse and how it affected me compounded the increasingly detrimental outcome.

Today, I feel liberated from the imprisonment. It took over forty-five years and hard work, but I made it!

I believe my journey was my destiny so I could be a beacon of hope for others who may be suffering within the same wickedness; victims and those who love them.

***

I certainly do not expect everyone to understand how I got "here". Each case is different, each victim is different, and it is imperative that parents never disregard that this abomination could happen to their own children. All genders, ages and socioeconomic groups can be affected. No one is exempt.

THERE IS HELP AVAILABLE.

My struggle is just one story and there are increasingly more nameless victims, male and female, who are attempting to write their own story in order to move forward. They may require therapy and treatment and possibly some help to get them there.

Listen to them without judgment, validate them with unconditional love and help them find proper diagnosis and treatment, when necessary.

Do whatever it takes to protect the child within them, starting now... even if they are an adult. Protect others by alerting law enforcement about the abuser, if applicable.

No one has the right to change another person's life in any negative manner.

Child sexual abuse is extremely ugly and damaging to a child. Abuse like this can be prevented, stopped and the damage can be helped to heal.

***

I *was a victim* of abuse.

I am now physically suffering the repercussions of all of the stress a body endures during such arduous trials. These lasting effects certainly are a constant reminder of all of the atrocities in which I was forced to be a guiltless participant.

Chapter 26 ~ Peace, Love and Awesomeness

I *am a survivor* of abuse.

I chose to take my power back.

My power is now.

My power is the future.

I have complete control of what I do with this experience.

My strength and willingness to survive and reduce my own suffering by being an active participant in my own healing helped me embrace the person I am today. I accept all I have experienced in life thus far. This acceptance helped me realize my life's purpose and learn to truly love myself. I finally discovered who I am…and I am awesome!

Your awesomeness exists, too. Sometimes we just need some help finding it.

I wish you peace, love and awesomeness!

Please feel free to contact me at CarrieWilliamsLee@yahoo.com, www.whowillsavemefromgrandpa.com, or find me on facebook as Carrie Williams-Lee, Author of "Who Will Save Me From Grandpa?"

There are many possible indicators of child sexual abuse, some of which I certainly experienced. Here is a list of some that I know I exhibited:

- Nightmares
- Loss of appetite
- Unusual aggressiveness to family or even pets
- Symptoms of trauma to genital areas, such as painful urination
- Bed wetting
- Showing unusual fear of a certain place or location
- Developing unexplained or frequent health problems
- Having episodes of panic, severe anxiety, flashbacks
- Reluctance to be alone with a certain person
- Self-abuse, such as hitting oneself or holding one's breath
- Decrease in school grades, withdrawn from normal, age appropriate activities
- Low self-esteem
- Depression
- Suicidal behavior

I feel that it is important for others to educate themselves about the indicators, especially since they may present themselves differently case by case. Please consult informational websites, mental health providers or physicians for this imperative information.

Here are some helpful websites:

www.protectkids.com
www.aacap.org
www.ptsd.va.gov/index.asp
www.psychiatry.org/patients-families/ptsd
www.stopitnow.org/ohc-content/warning-signs
www.drphil.com/articles/article/204
www.nmha.org